TEACHER'S PET PUBLICATIONS

LITPLAN TEACHER PACK
for
My Side of the Mountain
based on the book by
Jean Craighead George

Written by
Janine H. Sherman

© 1997 Teacher's Pet Publications
All Rights Reserved

This **LitPlan** for Jean Craighead George's
My Side of the Mountain
has been brought to you by Teacher's Pet Publications, Inc.

Copyright Teacher's Pet Publications 1997
11504 Hammock Point
Berlin MD 21811

Only the student materials in this unit plan (such as worksheets, study questions, and tests) may be reproduced multiple times for use in the purchaser's classroom.

For any additional copyright questions,
contact Teacher's Pet Publications.

www.tpet.com

TABLE OF CONTENTS - *My Side of the Mountain*

Introduction	5
Unit Objectives	8
Reading Assignment Sheet	9
Unit Outline	10
Study Questions (Short Answer)	13
Quiz/Study Questions (Multiple Choice)	24
Pre-reading Vocabulary Worksheets	43
Lesson One	63
Nonfiction Assignment Sheet	65
Oral Reading Evaluation Form	69
Writing Assignment 1	64
Writing Assignment 2	70
Writing Assignment 3	83
Writing Evaluation Form	72
Vocabulary Review Activities	89
Extra Writing Assignments/Discussion ?s	84
Unit Review Activities	91
Unit Tests	95
Unit Resource Materials	131
Vocabulary Resource Materials	147

A FEW NOTES ABOUT THE AUTHOR
Jean Craighead George

GEORGE, Jean Craighead (1919-). Jean Craighead George is the author of many outstanding books for children, including *Julie of the Wolves*, which won the Newbery Medal in 1973. *My Side of the Mountain*, first published in 1959, is a Newbery Honor Book, an ALA Notable Book, and a Hans Christian Anderson Award Honor Book.

Jean Craighead George's father was a naturalist and scientist. He taught her the plants and animals of the eastern forests and showed her where the wild edible fruits and tubers grew. On weekends along the Potomac River near Washington D.C., where she was born and grew up, she and her father boiled water in leaves and made rabbit traps. Her brothers are trained falconers and helped her train a falcon. As an elementary-age child, she attempted to run away and live peacefully in the wild, but returned after only forty minutes. Not so her hero, Sam Gribley, of *My Side of the Mountain*. Many children ask if there is a real Sam Gribley, and her response is " there is no real Sam, except inside me."

Jean carries little spiral notebooks with her on her forays into the natural world. She claims to take notes all the time. An accomplished artist who has illustrated many of her own books, Jean also sketches as she hikes. She calls her first drafts "first runs" in which she gets to know all the people and see how they're moving. She lets the movie run in her head, and then goes back and edits it in later drafts.

Jean feels that children are her audience and she wants to grab them on the first page, if possible, and keep them to the last page. Other outstanding books written by her include: *The Summer of the Falcon, The Wounded Wolf, The Talking Earth, One Day in the Prairie, Water Sky, Shark Beneath the Reef, The First Thanksgiving*, and *On The Far Side of the Mountain*; sequel to *My Side of the Mountain*.

INTRODUCTION - *My Side of the Mountain*

This unit has been designed to develop students' reading, writing, thinking, and language skills through exercises and activities related to *My Side of the Mountain* by Jean Craighead George. It includes twenty lessons, supported by extra resource materials.

The **introductory lesson** exposes students to the setting of the novel, the Catskill Mountain, New York area. It also doubles as the first writing assignment for the unit. Following the introductory activity, students are given an explanation of how the activity relates to the book they are about to read. Following the transition, students are given the materials they will be using during the unit.

The **reading assignments** are approximately twenty-five pages each; some are a little shorter while others are a little longer. Students have approximately 15 minutes of pre-reading work to do prior to each reading assignment. This pre-reading work involves reviewing the study questions for the assignment and doing some vocabulary work for 8 to 10 vocabulary words they will encounter in their reading.

The **study guide questions** are fact-based questions; students can find the answers to these questions right in the text. These questions come in two formats: short answer or multiple choice. The best use of these materials is probably to use the short answer version of the questions as study guides for students (since answers will be more complete), and to use the multiple choice version for occasional quizzes. It might be a good idea to make transparencies of your answer keys for the overhead projector.

The **vocabulary work** is intended to enrich students' vocabularies as well as to aid in the students' understanding of the book. Prior to each reading assignment, students will complete a two-part worksheet for approximately 8 to 10 vocabulary words in the upcoming reading assignment. Part I focuses on students' use of general knowledge and contextual clues by giving the sentence in which the word appears in the text. Students are then to write down what they think the words mean based on the words' usage. Part II nails down the definitions of the words by giving students dictionary definitions of the words and having students match the words to the correct definitions based on the words' contextual usage. Students should then have an understanding of the words when they meet them in the text.

After each reading assignment, students will go back and formulate answers for the study guide questions. Discussion of these questions serves as a **review** of the most important events and ideas presented in the reading assignments.

After students complete extra discussion questions, there is a **vocabulary review** lesson which pulls together all of the fragmented vocabulary lists for the reading assignments and gives students a review of all of the words they have studied.

Following the reading of the book, two lessons are devoted to the **extra discussion questions/writing assignments**. These questions focus on interpretation, critical analysis and personal response, employing a variety of thinking skills and adding to the students' understanding of the novel. These questions are done as a **group activity**. Using the information they have acquired so far through individual work and class discussions, students get together to further examine the text and to brainstorm ideas relating to the themes of the novel.

The group activity is followed by a **reports and discussion** session in which the groups share their ideas about the book with the entire class; thus, the entire class gets exposed to many different ideas regarding the themes and events of the book.

There are three **writing assignments** in this unit, each with the purpose of informing, persuading, or having students express personal opinions. The first assignment is writing to inform: students will draw from the information gained in their research on the Catskills, to write a descriptive composition on the setting. The second assignment gives students the opportunity to express their personal ideas: students will apply the technique of flashback by composing their own personal autobiographical flashback. The third assignment is to give students a chance to persuade: students will assume Sam's identity and try to convince his parents to take the rest of the family home and allow him to remain on Bitter Mountain, *alone* and living off the land.

In addition, there is a **nonfiction reading assignment**. Students are required to read a piece of nonfiction related in some way to *My Side of the Mountain*. After reading their nonfiction pieces, students will fill out a worksheet on which they answer questions regarding facts, interpretation, criticism, and personal opinions. During one class period, students make **oral presentations** about the nonfiction pieces they have read. This not only exposes all students to a wealth of information, it also gives students the opportunity to practice **public speaking**.

There is an optional **class project** (Project Survival) through which students can utilize and apply information learned through reading the novel to construct a wilderness survival guide.

The **review lesson** pulls together all of the aspects of the unit. The teacher is given four or five choices of activities or games to use which all serve the same basic function of reviewing all of the information presented in the unit.

The **unit test** comes in two formats: all multiple choice-matching-true/false or with a mixture of matching, short answer, and composition. As a convenience, two different tests for each format have been included.

There are additional **support materials** included with this unit. The **Unit Resource section** includes suggestions for an in-class library, crossword and word search puzzles related to the novel, and extra vocabulary worksheets. There is a list of **bulletinboard ideas** which gives the teacher suggestions for bulletinboards to go along with this unit. In addition, there is a list of **extra class activities** the teacher could choose from to enhance the unit or as a substitution for an exercise the teacher might feel is inappropriate for his/her class. **Answer keys** are located directly after the **reproducible student materials** throughout the unit. The student materials may be reproduced for use in the teacher's classroom without infringement of copyrights. No other portion of this unit may be reproduced without the written consent of Teacher's Pet Publications, Inc.

UNIT OBJECTIVES - *My Side of the Mountain*

1. Through reading *My Side of the Mountain*, students will gain understanding of the themes of survival, courage, and companionship.

2. Students will develop an awareness of Sam's individuality and examine their own.

3. Students will do background research on the Catskill Mountain, New York, area to provide meaning to the geographical references made by the author.

4. Students will gain appreciation for and demonstrate proficiency in identifying and using figurative language.

5. Students will demonstrate their understanding of the text on four levels: factual, interpretive, critical and personal.

6. Students will be given the opportunity to practice reading aloud and silently to improve their skills in each area.

7. Students will answer questions to demonstrate their knowledge and understanding of the main events and characters in *My Side of the Mountain* as they relate to the author's theme development.

8. Students will enrich their vocabularies and improve their understanding of the novel through the vocabulary lessons prepared for use in conjunction with the novel.

9. The writing assignments in this unit are geared to several purposes:
    a. To have students demonstrate their abilities to inform, to persuade, or to express their own personal ideas
        Note: Students will demonstrate ability to write effectively to <u>inform</u> by developing and organizing facts to convey information. Students will demonstrate the ability to write effectively to <u>persuade</u> by selecting and organizing relevant information, establishing an argumentative purpose, and by designing an appropriate strategy for an identified audience. Students will demonstrate the ability to write effectively to <u>express personal ideas</u> by selecting a form and its appropriate elements.
    b. To check the students' reading comprehension
    c. To make students think about the ideas presented by the novel
    d. To encourage logical thinking

READING ASSIGNMENT SHEET - *My Side of the Mountain*

Date Assigned	Reading Assignment (Chapters)	Completion Date
	Set 1 I Hole Up in a Snowstorm I Get Started on This Venture I Find Gribley's Farm	
	Set 2 I Find Many Useful Plants The Old, Old Tree I Meet One of My Kind and Have a Terrible Time Getting Away The King's Provider What I Did About the First Man Who Was After Me	
	Set 3 I Learn to Season My Food How a Door Came to Me Frightful Learns Her ABC's I Find a Real Live Man	
	Set 4 The Autumn Provides Food and Loneliness	
	Set 5 We All Learn About Halloween I Find Out What to Do About Hunters	
	Set 6 Trouble Begins	
	Set 7 I Pile Up Wood and Go on with Winter I Learn About Birds and People I Have a Good Look at Winter and Find Spring in the Snow	
	Set 8 The Spring in the Winter and the Beginning of My Story's End I Cooperate with the Ending The City Comes to Me	

UNIT OUTLINE - *My Side of the Mountain*

1 Library Nonfiction Assignment	2 Work Session Writing Assignment 1	3 Introduction Materials PVR Set 1	4 Study ?s Set 1 PVR Set 2 Oral Rdg Eval Writing Assignment 2	5 Study ?s Set 2 Work Session on W.A. #2 Writing Conference
6 Survival Problem Solving PVR Set 3	7 Study ?s Set 3 PVR Set 4	8 Study ?'s Set 4 PVR Set 5	9 Study ?'s Set 5 Companionship PVR Set 6	10 Study ?'s Set 6 Newspaper articles
11 Group Activity Figurative Language PV Set 7	12 Read Set 7 Study ?'s Set 7 PVR Set 8	13 Study ?'s Set 8 Individuality	14 Writing Assignment 3	15 Extra Discussion Questions
16 Extra Discussion ?'s / Writing Assignment Sharing	17 Vocabulary Review	18 Review	19 Test	20 Project Survival

Key: P = Preview Study Questions   V = Vocabulary Work   R = Read

STUDY GUIDE QUESTIONS

SHORT ANSWER STUDY GUIDE QUESTIONS - *My Side of the Mountain*

Set #1 "I Hole Up in a Snowstorm"," I Get Started on This Venture", and "I Find Gribley's Farm"

1. During what time of year does this story begin?
2. How does Sam know the date?
3. For how many months has Sam been away from home?
4. Where does Sam make his home?
5. In what ways does Sam prepare for the coming of winter in the forest?
6. What was the first sign of the upcoming blizzard?
7. Why had the Gribley farm been abandoned?
8. Name the items Sam took with him from New York.
9. How did Sam get from his home to the Catskill area?
10. Sam is able to remember certain things by doing what?
11. Relate Sam's first night in the woods.
12. Who was Bill?
13. How does Mrs. Turner help Sam?
14. Compare Sam's second night in the forest to his first.

Set #2 "I Find Many Useful Plants", "The Old, Old Tree", "I Meet One of My Kind and Have a Terrible Time Getting Away", "The King's Provider", and "What I Did About the First Man Who Was After Me"

1. What important information did Sam learn from a manual about the outdoors?
2. When Sam couldn't find any fish to eat, what did he do?
3. Sam values which type of trees the most?
4. How does he know the boundary of his great-grandfather's farm?
5. Why does Sam choose a hemlock tree for his home?
6. Sam becomes distraught while working on his new tree home. Why?
7. Explain how Sam is able to cook the crow eggs he finds.
8. While stamping out his lunch fire, what idea comes to Sam?
9. Who surprises Sam as he is constructing his bed?
10. After assisting the elderly lady home, where does Sam decide to go?
11. Who is Frightful?
12. Why had the fire warden shown up on Sam's mountain?

My Side of the Mountain Short Answer Study Questions Page 2

Set #3 "I Learn to Season My Food", "How a Door Came to Me", and "Frightful Learns Her ABC's"

1. What puzzles Sam about animal trapping?
2. Who is the Baron?
3. How does Sam learn to season his food?
4. How is Sam able to get a deer?
5. Sam is pleased to learn this about earthworms.
6. List the ways Sam uses the deer he found.
7. How does Sam train Frightful?
8. Explain how Sam traps his own deer.
9. Describe the clothing Sam makes from the deerhide.
10. Why does Sam take away the first sparrow Frightful catches?

Set #4 "I Find a Real Live Man"

1. Describe Sam's manner of summer bathing.
2. Who is Jesse Coon James?
3. How does Frightful alert Sam to the change in the forest?
4. Who is Bando?
5. Why does Bando go to town?
6. How does Bando use the clay they found along the stream bank?
7. Explain how Bando made the willow whistles.
8. Cite the change in Sam's feelings after his visitor leaves.

Set #5 " The Autumn Provides Food and Loneliness", "We All Learn About Halloween", " I Find Out What to Do With Hunters"

1. What changes did autumn bring to the mountain?
2. How does Sam get clay for his fireplace home from the stream bank?
3. How does Sam come across the stone he needed for his fireplace?
4. What was the primary problem Sam encountered while trying out his new clay furnace?
5. What animals does Sam think send messages to each other in the forest?
6. How does Sam save apples for the winter?
7. Are the Baron and Frightful good friends?
8. In what way did Sam's Halloween party backfire?
9. Sam had a close call with the hunter. Explain.
10. What trouble did Sam have tanning the hides of the last two deer?

My Side of the Mountain Short Answer Study Questions Page 3

Set #6 "Trouble Begins", "I Pile Up Wood and Go on with Winter", and "I Learn About Birds and People"

1. Why do Sam and Frightful go to the spring?
2. Where does Sam find himself walking to on Sunday?
3. Who is Mr. Jacket?
4. Upon returning from town, what does Sam realize is the one thing he hasn't done to prepare for winter?
5. How did Sam spend his winter days and nights?
6. With whom in the forest does Sam compare his Third Avenue, New York neighbors?
7. What news does Bando bring when he comes for his Christmas visit?
8. Who surprised Bando and Sam on Christmas Day?
9. What is his father's reaction to his living situation?
10. Why does his father come back and leave by a different route?

Set # 7 "I Have a Good Look at Winter and Find Spring in the Snow"

1. What does Sam design to help him travel on foot in the snow?
2. Name the animal that Sam called his barometer to the upcoming weather.
3. Why does Sam say there is no such thing as a "still winter night"?
4. What was the most disturbing part of the ice storm?
5. How long did it take for the forest to arise after the ice storm?
6. What vitamin did Sam lack and how did he get it?
7. How does Sam help the deer in January?

Set #8 "The Spring in the Winter and the Beginning of My Story's End", "I Cooperate with the Ending", "The City Comes to Me"

1. How many cups of sap does it take to make one cup of syrup?
2. Who is Matt Spell?
3. What bargain does Sam agree to so Matt Spell won't write an article about him?
4. How is Sam able to talk things out without anyone there talk things over with?
5. Who is Aaron?
6. Who else shows up to spend spring vacation with Sam?
7. How does Sam know he is no longer a runaway?
8. Who becomes a regular weekend guest?
9. While Sam is relaxing in the sunny meadow one June day, who intrudes upon him?
10. What does the title of the last chapter "The City Comes to Me" mean?

ANSWER KEY: SHORT ANSWER STUDY QUESTIONS - *My Side of the Mountain*

Set #1   "I Hole Up in a Snowstorm"," I Get Started on This Venture", and "I Find Gribley's Farm"

1. During what time of year does this story begin?
    It begins in the winter in early December.

2. How does Sam know the date?
    Sam makes notches in an aspen pole to mark each day as it passes. It is his calendar.

3. For how many months has Sam been away from home?
    He has been away from home for eight months.

4. Where does Sam make his home?
    He makes it in a huge hemlock tree trunk.

5. In what ways does Sam prepare for the coming of winter in the forest?
    He learns how to make a fire, finds plants to eat, traps animals, and catches fish.

6. What was the first sign of the upcoming blizzard?
    While Sam was smoking fish in the early morning, the sky was very dark.

7. Why had the Gribley farm been abandoned?
    The farm had failed so his great-grandfather went to sea.

8. Name the items Sam took with him from New York.
    He took a penknife, a ball of cord, an ax, and 40 dollars.

9. How did Sam get from his home to the Catskill area?
    He took a train.

10. When Sam needs to remember something what does he do?
    He jots down notes on various things such as scraps of paper or bark.

11. Relate Sam's first night in the woods.
    He was scared, tired, and very hungry. His fire failed and he chose the wrong place for his bed. He was quite discouraged.

My Side of the Mountain Study Guide Question Answers page 2

12. Who was Bill?
    He was an old man that lived near the road in a woodstove-warmed house. He fed Sam and taught him how to make a proper fire.

13. How does Mrs. Turner help Sam?
    She finds books and maps about Delaware County which include the Gribley farm. They guide him to the correct location of his family's property.

14. Compare Sam's second night in the forest to his first.
    He makes a successful fire and eats his fill of catfish. He felt very independent.

Set #2 "I Find Many Useful Plants", "The Old, Old Tree", "I Meet One of My Kind and Have a Terrible Time Getting Away", "The King's Provider", and "What I Did About the First Man Who Was After Me"

1. What important information did Sam learn from a manual about the outdoors?
   Watch what the birds and animals are eating to learn what is edible and what is not edible.

2. When Sam couldn't find any fish to eat, what did he do?
   He dug up mussels and steamed them.

3. Sam values which type of trees the most and how does he remember where they are located on the property?
   He values the hickory, walnut and apple the most. He marks x's on his map he made of the property on his road map.

4. How does he know the boundary of his great-grandfather's farm?
   It is outlined by a stone wall.

5. Why does Sam choose a hemlock tree for his home?
   He admires its size and location.

6. Sam becomes distraught while working on his new tree home. Why?
   He has totally forgotten to plan ahead for his next meal and is very tired from working on his home.

7. Explain how Sam is able to cook the crow eggs he finds.
   He sews together a skunk cabbage leaf to form a cup and then boils the eggs in it.

My Side of the Mountain Study Guide Question Answers page 3

8. While stamping out his lunch fire, what idea comes to Sam?
    He could use fire to burn out his tree trunk like the Indians burnt out canoes.

9. Who surprises Sam as he is constructing his bed?
    A little old lady looking for her annual strawberry patch.

10. After assisting the elderly lady home, where does Sam decide to go?
    He heads for the library to look up books on falcons, as he is aware of a falcon nest nearby.

11. Who is Frightful?
    She is the baby falcon that Sam takes from the nest to raise and train.

12. Why had the fire warden shown up on Sam's mountain?
    It was very dry and apparently some of Sam's fires must have been spotted.

Set #3 "I Learn to Season My Food", "How a Door Came to Me", and "Frightful Learns Her ABC's"

1. What puzzles Sam about animal trapping?
    He can't believe animals don't question why delicious food is in such a ridiculous spot.

2. Who is the Baron?
    He is frisky weasel that Sam catches in a trap who is totally unafraid of Sam and even berates him for trapping him.

3. How does Sam learn to season his food?
    He boils hickory sticks to get the salty residue for seasoning.

4. How is Sam able to get a deer?
    He dragged a dead deer shot by a hunter into the woods and covered it with hemlock boughs to camouflage it till the hunter moved on.

5. Sam is pleased to learn this about earthworms.
    They make a pip, pop, pop, pop sound.

6. List the ways Sam uses the deer he found.
    He uses the hide for a door, jesses for Frightful, and candle wicks. He smoked the meat and used bones for a spearhead.

My Side of the Mountain Study Guide Question Answers page 4

7. How does Sam train Frightful?
    She does not eat unless she first flies to Sam's wrist.

8. Explain how Sam traps his own deer.
    He constructs a figure-four trap under a log baited with a ball of hickory salt and turtle fat.

9. Describe the clothing Sam makes from the deerhide.
    He fashions pants and a big, square pocket vest to use to gather food.

10. Why does Sam take away the first sparrow Frightful catches?
    If she gets in the habit of eating what she catches she'll go wild.

Set #4 "I Find a Real Live Man"

1. Describe Sam's manner of summer bathing.
    He bathes in the cool spring water huddled between moss and ferns scrubbing with the bark of a slippery elm.

2. Who is Jesse Coon James?
    He is a mountain raccoon Sam adopts.

3. How does Frightful alert Sam to the change in the forest?
    She dug her talons into Sam's shoulder tensing up swiftly.

4. Who is Bando?
    He is a college English teacher that became lost in the forest. Sam thinks he is an escaped criminal.

5. Why does Bando go to town?
    He buys 5 pounds of sugar to make blueberry jam.

6. How does Bando use the clay they found along the stream bank?
    He makes pottery in which to store their jam.

7. Explain how Bando made the willow whistles.
    He cut two fat eight inch twigs, slipped the bark, made a mouthpiece at one end, cut a hole beneath it, and used the wood to slide up and down like a trombone.

My Side of the Mountain Study Guide Question Answers page 5

8. Cite the change in Sam's feelings after his visitor leaves.
 Sam is now lonesome for human contact.

Set #5 "The Autumn Provides Food and Loneliness", "We All Learn About Halloween", " I Find Out What to Do With Hunters"

1. What changes did autumn bring to the mountain?
 The grasses were seeded, and squirrels and chipmunks were collecting and hiding nuts.

2. How does Sam get clay for his fireplace home from the stream bank?
 He loads up his pants and drags them home full of clay looking like a scarecrow.

3. How does Sam come across the stone he needed for his fireplace?
 When he grabbed Frightful's jesses tightly, he hit his hand on a rock- the exact type stone he needed.

4. What was the primary problem Sam encountered while trying out his new clay furnace?
 It was ventilation. The fire took all the oxygen out of his tree home.

5. What animals does Sam think send messages to each other in the forest?
 Squirrels signaling to each other where the best gathering of nuts is.

6. How does Sam save apples for the winter?
 He cuts them into slices and dries them on a boulder in the sun.

7. Are the Baron and Frightful good friends?
 No, Frightful is very wary of the rascally Baron.

8. In what way did Sam's Halloween party backfire?
 The animals took over. He was sprayed by a skunk, and his hard won cache of food was discovered. Morale: Don't feed wild animals!

9. Sam had a close call with the hunter. Explain.
 In deerskin clothing, he was mistaken for a deer and a bullet came very close to him.

10. What trouble did Sam have tanning the hides of the last two deer?
 The water in the oak tree stump, where he soaked the hides in tannic acid, kept freezing.

My Side of the Mountain Study Guide Question Answers page 6

Set #6 "Trouble Begins", "I Pile Up Wood and Go on with Winter",and "I Learn About Birds and People"

1. Why do Sam and Frightful go to the spring?
    To look into the mirrored reflection in the water.

2. Where does Sam find himself walking to on Sunday?
    He ends up at the local drugstore.

3. Who is Mr. Jacket?
    A young man, thirteen or fourteen Sam met in the drugstore in the comic book section. He is\ wearing a leather jacket.

4. Upon returning from town, what does Sam realize is the one thing he hasn't done to prepare for winter?
    He hasn't stacked a big wood pile.

5. How did Sam spend his winter days and nights?
    He ice fished, hunted with Frightful, cooked, and sewed.

6. With whom in the forest does Sam compare his Third Avenue, New York neighbors?
    He compares his former neighbors with the chickadees.

7. What news does Bando bring when he comes for his Christmas visit?
    There are newspaper clippings from New York newspapers.

8. Who surprised Bando and Sam on Christmas Day?
    Sam's father showed up.

9. What is his father's reaction to his living situation?
    He is thrilled, proud, and amazed with his son.

10. Why does his father come back and leave by a different route?
    He doesn't want anyone to track him and find Sam to spoil his lifestyle.

My Side of the Mountain Study Guide Question Answers page 7

Set # 7 "I Have a Good Look at Winter and Find Spring in the Snow", pgs. 131-148

1. What does Sam design to help him travel on foot in the snow?
    He makes snowshoes of ash slats.

2. Name the animal that Sam called his barometer to the upcoming weather.
    He calls the nuthatch his barometer. If he sees him holing up, Sam does too.

3. Why does Sam say there is no such thing as a "still winter night"?
    The trees cry out, winds scream, and animals scurry all through the night.

4. What was the most disturbing part of the ice storm?
    The sound of the exploding trees.

5. How long did it take for the forest to arise after the ice storm?
    It took three days.

6. What vitamin did Sam lack and how did he get it?
    He was lacking vitamin C and got it by eating rabbit liver.

7. How does Sam help the deer in January?
    He climbed trees and cut down tender limbs for them to eat.

Set #8 "The Spring in the Winter and the Beginning of My Story's End", "I Cooperate with the Ending", "The City Comes to Me"

1. How many cups of sap does it take to make one cup of syrup?
    It takes thirty-two cups of sap to make one cup of syrup.

2. Who is Matt Spell?
    He is a young reporter from the Poughkeepsie New Yorker looking for the wild boy to write an article about him.

3. What bargain does Sam agree to so Matt Spell won't write an article about him?
    He agrees to allow Matt to spend his spring vacation with him starting April 12.

4. How is Sam able to talk things out without anyone there to talk things over with?
    He holds forums in his head with his dad and friends each giving him their advice.

My Side of the Mountain Study Guide Question Answers page 8

5. Who is Aaron?
   He is a New York songwriter to which Sam gives his bird song impressions.

6. Who else shows up to spend spring vacation with Sam?
   Bando

7. How does Sam know he is no longer a runaway?
   Bando and Matt make a guest home from one of the other trees.

8. Who becomes a regular weekend guest?
   Mr. Jacket (Tom Sidler) comes up frequently to stay with Sam.

9. While Sam is relaxing in the sunny meadow one June day, who intrudes upon him?
   Photographers shooting pictures of the wild boy.

10. What does the title of the last chapter "The City Comes to Me" mean?
    His family comes from the city to live in the woods with him.

MULTIPLE CHOICE STUDY/QUIZ QUESTIONS - *My Side of the Mountain*

Set #1 "I Hole Up in a Snowstorm"," I Get Started on This Venture", and "I Find Gribley's Farm

1. This story begins during the
    a. winter.
    b. summer.
    c. spring.
    d. fall.

2. Sam is able to know the current date by
    a. using a sundial he found.
    b. looking at the pocket calendar he brought along.
    c. making notches in an aspen pole for each day since he left home.
    d. determining the position of the moon and stars.

3. Sam has been away from home for
    a. one month.
    b. eight months.
    c. two weeks.
    d. eight weeks.

4. Sam decides to make his home out of
    a. the former foundation of his great-grandfathers farm house.
    b. an abandoned cave.
    c. a run down hunter's cabin.
    d. a huge hemlock tree trunk.

5. Sam prepares for winter in the forest by
    a. learning how to make a fire.
    b. finding edible plants.
    c. trapping animals and catching fish.
    d. all of the above

6. The first sign of the impending blizzard was
    a. the sudden chill in the air.
    b. the sound of the animals holing up.
    c. the dark sky in the early morning.
    d. all of the above

My Side of the Mountain Study/Quiz Questions Multiple Choice Format Page 2

7. The Gribley farm had been abandoned because
    a. it had failed and his great-grandfather went to sea.
    b. of the forest fire that destroyed the mountain.
    c. the Civil War had taken his great-grandfather away to war.
    d. none of the above

8. Which of the following items *didn't* Sam take with him on his journey?
    a. a penknife
    b. field guides
    c. a ball of cord
    d. money

9. Sam traveled from New York City to the Catskill area by
    a. hitching rides on produce trucks.
    b. walking part of the way and running the rest of the way.
    c. riding on a Greyhound bus.
    d. taking a train.

10. Where does Sam write down the things he wants to remember?
    a. He writes on scraps of paper.
    b. He types it into his personal notepad.
    c. He jots it down on pieces of bark.
    d. Both A and C

11. Which set of adjectives best describe Sam's feeling about his first night in the forest?
    a. scared, tired, hungry
    b. excited, hungry, confident
    c. curious, tired, anxious
    d. nervous, exhausted, warm

12. How does Bill help Sam?
    a. He feeds Sam.
    b. He teaches Sam how to make a proper fire.
    c. He goes with Sam to be sure he can get along OK.
    d. Both A and B

13. Mrs. Turner is the local school teacher in Delhi.
    a. true
    b. false

My Side of the Mountain Study/Quiz Questions Multiple Choice Format Page 3

Set #2 "I Find Many Useful Plants", "The Old, Old Tree", "I Meet One of My Kind and Have a Terrible Time Getting Away","The King's Provider", and "What I Did About the First Man Who Was After Me"

1. What important information did Sam learn from a manual about the outdoors?
    a. How to determine the best place to make a bed.
    b. Watch what the birds and animals are eating to learn what is edible and what is not.
    c. The best way to make a fire in the forest.
    d. none of the above

2. When Sam could not catch any fish for his meal he
    a. dug up mussels and steamed them.
    b. trapped a rabbit and cooked it.
    c. made a salad of dandelion greens and robin eggs.
    d. boiled acorns until tender and then mashed them.

3. Sam values which type of trees the most ?
    a. hickory
    b. walnut
    c. apple
    d. all of the above

4. How does Sam know the boundary of his great-grandfather's farm?
    a. It has a grove of hemlocks on all four corners.
    b. It is the only farm in the area.
    c. It is outlined by a stone wall.
    d. There are barbed wire fences surrounding the property lines.

5. Why does Sam choose a hemlock tree for his home?
    a. He admires its size.
    b. He thinks no one would find him there.
    c. He is thrilled with its location.
    d. all of the above

6. Why does Sam become disturbed with himself while working on his new home?
    a. He has not planned ahead for his next meal.
    b. He is tired and doesn't want to have to stop and find food.
    c. He thinks he has chosen a poor spot for his home.
    d. both A and B

My Side of the Mountain Study/Quiz Questions Multiple Choice Format Page 4

7. Sam is able to cook the crow eggs he finds by
    a. putting them in the sun and baking them.
    b. sewing together a skunk cabbage leaf to form a cup and boiling the eggs in it.
    c. dropping them gently into the bubbling, hot spring water.
    d. scrambling them and frying them on a hot stone.

8. Sam realized he can use fire like the Indians did to
    a. to send smoke signals in an emergency.
    b. to cook and smoke his animals and fish
    c. burn out the interior of his hemlock tree trunk home.
    d. all of the above

9. Who surprises Sam as he is constructing his bed?
    a. The fire warden looking for the remains of Sam's recent fires.
    b. His father has come looking for him.
    c. A lost hobo is looking for a place to hide out for awhile.
    d. A little old lady who is looking for her annual strawberry patch.

10. After assisting the elderly lady home, Sam decides to go
    a. to the local library.
    b. to Bill's house to share his discoveries with him.
    c. into the lady's house for some strawberry jam.
    d. on the other side of the mountain to look around for his next place to trap.

11. Who is Frightful?
    a. He is a frisky raccoon that bothers Sam.
    b. She is the baby falcon that Sam takes from a nest to raise and train.
    c. He is a snake that frightens Sam.
    d. She is a deer that watches Sam's movements.

12. The fire warden shows up on Sam's mountain to bring him home to his parents.
    a. true
    b. false

My Side of the Mountain Study/Quiz Questions Multiple Choice Format Page 5

Set #3 "I Learn to Season My Food", "How a Door Came to Me", and "Frightful Learns Her ABC's"

1. What puzzles Sam about animal trapping?
    a. He can't understand how to make the trap work properly.
    b. He can't believe the animals aren't suspicious about the delicious food found in silly places.
    c. He isn't sure where to place the traps.
    d. Both B and C

2. The Baron is
    a. is frisky weasel that Sam catches in a trap.
    b. a beautiful falcon that Sam trains.
    c. a slinky snake that appears one day.
    d. a scrawny raccoon that falls into the stream while Sam is bathing.

3. Sam seasons his food with
    a. herbs and spices he digs up in the forest.
    b. spicy arrowroot.
    c. sunflower seeds.
    d. the salty residue from hickory sticks.

4. Sam is able to get a deer because
    a. the hunter lost the scent and went the wrong way.
    b. it fell into his trap right after it was shot by the hunter.
    c. the hunter shot two deer and forgot about the first one.
    d. he camouflages it with hickory boughs so the hunter can't find it.

5. Sam is pleased to learn that earthworms
    a. communicate with each other.
    b. live in a group.
    c. make a pip, pop, pop, pop sound.
    d. all of the above

6. Sam uses the deer for
    a. candle wicks.
    b. leg straps for Frightful.
    c. a door
    d. all of the above

My Side of the Mountain Study/Quiz Questions Multiple Choice Format Page 6

7. How does Sam train Frightful?
    a. He throws food into the air for her to fetch.
    b. She must listen for his whistle before she lands.
    c. He counts to ten and then she must land on his shoulder.
    d. She does not eat unless she first flies to Sam's wrist.

8. Explain how Sam traps his own deer.
    a. He constructs a figure-four trap under a log baited with a ball of hickory salt and turtle fat.
    b. He follows hunters and waits until they are close to a deer and then drops a net over them.
    c. He designs a metal trap from the implements in the old farm foundation.
    d. He lures them with a hickory wood fire and then bags them.

9. Which of the following *doesn't* Sam make from the deer he traps?
    a. pants
    b. pocket vest to carry food
    c. bone needle
    d. shirt

10. Sam takes away the first sparrow Frightful catches.
    a. true
    b. false

My Side of the Mountain Study/Quiz Questions Multiple Choice Format Page 7

Set #4 "I Find a Real Live Man"

1. Describe Sam's manner of summer bathing.
    a. He waits until there is an afternoon shower and then stands out in the meadow.
    b. He jumps in the pond and swims with the frogs.
    c. He bathes in the cool spring water scrubbing with the bark of a slippery elm.

2. Jesse Coon James is
    a. is frisky weasel that Sam catches in a trap.
    b. a beautiful falcon that Sam trains.
    c. a slinky snake that appears one day.
    d. a scrawny raccoon that falls into the stream while Sam is bathing.

3. Frightful alerts Sam to the change in the forest by
    a. digging her talons into Sam's shoulder.
    b. flitting her wings furiously.
    c. flying up above him and hovering above the disturbance.
    d. all of the above

4. Bando is
    a. the hunter who lost his deer.
    b. a lost college English professor.
    c. a bandit who has escaped the law.
    d. a high school biology teacher.

5. Bando goes to town to
    a. get a haircut.
    b. find books at the library about pottery.
    c. buy a five pound bag of sugar for blueberry jam.

6. Bando uses the clay they find along the stream bank to
    a. make pottery in which to store their jam.
    b. make adobe bricks for a new home.
    c. form artistic sculptures of the animals in the forest.
    d. create a stove in which to bake acorn bread.

My Side of the Mountain Study/Quiz Questions Multiple Choice Format Page 8

7. Select the one item not associated with Bando's wind whistles.
	a. They are trombone-like.
	b. They are made from willow reeds.
	c. They have a mouthpiece.
	d. They play sad songs best.

8. Sam is relieved when his visitor leaves.
	a. true
	b. false

My Side of the Mountain Study/Quiz Questions Multiple Choice Format Page 9

Set #5 " The Autumn Provides Food and Loneliness", "We All Learn About Halloween", " I Find Out What to Do With Hunters"

1. Which of the following were not changes autumn brought to the mountain?
    a. grasses were burned and seeded
    b. squirrels were collecting and hiding nuts
    c. leaves were as green as grass
    d. birds were ready to fly south

2. Sam gets clay for his fireplace home from the stream bank by
    a. loading up a wheelbarrow and wheeling it home.
    b. filling his pants and dragging them home.
    c. carrying handfuls back to a tree stump.
    d. cramming it in all his pockets and taking it along with him.

3. Sam finds the stone he needed for his fireplace by
    a. accident.
    b. searching the forest for days.
    c. Frightful landing on it.
    d. lifting it out of the stream after watching a frog land on it.

4. Sam's primary problem with his new clay furnace was
    a. getting the clay to stand up.
    b. keeping the ashes out of the way.
    c. ventilation.
    d. the size of the mouth.

5. Sam thinks the squirrels send messages to each other in the forest.
    a. true
    b. false

6. Sam saves apples for the winter by
    a. cutting them up into slices.
    b. drying them in the sun.
    c. storing them in his food tree.
    d. all of the above

My Side of the Mountain Study/Quiz Questions Multiple Choice Format Page 10

7. The Baron and Frightful have become good friends.
    a. true
    b. false

8. The moral of Sam's Halloween party was
    a. Don't feed wild animals.
    b. You never know what a weasel will do next.
    c. The full moon causes unearthly events.
    d. Skunks will appear when you least expect them.

9. Sam had a close call with the hunter because
    a. he was in the wrong place at the wrong time.
    b. Frightful drew the hunter's attention.
    c. he was confused and didn't know hunting season had started.
    d. his clothing resembled a deer.

10. Sam had difficulty tanning the hides of the last two deer because
    a. they were so large.
    b. the water in the oak stump kept freezing.
    c. the deerhide was too tough to work with easily.
    d. he had trouble skinning the hides.

My Side of the Mountain Study/Quiz Questions Multiple Choice Format Page 11

Set #6 "Trouble Begins", "I Pile Up Wood and Go on with Winter", and "I Learn About Birds and People"

1. What do Sam and Frightful see at the spring?
    a. They see the trout they have been eyeing.
    b. They see a snapping turtle that would make tasty soup.
    c. They see their reflection in the water.
    d. The see the raccoon digging up mussels.

2. Sam finds himself walking on Sunday to
    a. the library.
    b. the drugstore.
    c. the local Catholic church.
    d. to the strawberry picker's house.

3. Mr. Jacket is
    a. the man behind the counter at the store.
    b. a motorcycle rider from the nearest town.
    c. a young man in a leather jacket from town.
    d. a hobo looking for a fire and a place to rest.

4. Upon returning from town, Sam realizes he hasn't
    a. stacked a big wood pile.
    b. stored enough fruit.
    c. hidden his stash of food well enough.
    d. written to his mother.

5. Which of the following *doesn't* Sam do with his winter days and nights?
    a. ice fish
    b. hunt
    c. cook
    d. write music

6. Sam compares his Third Avenue, New York neighbors with whom in the forest?
    a. red-eyed vireos
    b. nuthatches
    c. squirrels
    d. chickadees

My Side of the Mountain Study/Quiz Questions Multiple Choice Format Page 12

7. Bando brings newspaper clippings of
   a. the wild boy living in the forest.
   b. the great New York City fire.
   c. the prediction of the upcoming blizzard.
   d. his academic award at the college.

8. Sam's father shows up on Christmas Day.
   a. true
   b. false

9. Which set of adjectives best describe Sam's father's reaction to his son's adventure?
   a. worried, nervous, disappointed
   b. excited, thrilled, apprehensive
   c. proud, amazed, thrilled
   d. furious, agitated, worried

10. His father returns and then leaves by a different route because
    a. he forgot which way to go and needed Sam's help.
    b. he didn't want anyone following him.
    c. the storm caused the original route to be closed.
    d. he wanted to come back and tell Sam goodbye.

My Side of the Mountain Study/Quiz Questions Multiple Choice Format Page 13

Set # 7 "I Have a Good Look at Winter and Find Spring in the Snow", pgs. 131-148

1. Sam designs these to help him travel easier in the snow.
    a. snowshoes
    b. skis
    c. sleds
    d. sleighs

2. Name the animal that Sam called his barometer to the upcoming weather.
    a. red vireo
    b. chipmunk
    c. possum
    d. nuthatch

3. Sam says there is no such thing as a "still winter night" because
    a. the trees cry out
    b. the winds scream
    c. animals scurry
    d. all of the above

4. What was the most disturbing part of the ice storm?
    a. The sound of the exploding trees.
    b. The cracking of the stream.
    c. The lack of light into the tree.
    d. The silence in the forest.

5. It took _____ for the forest to arise after the ice storm.
    a. one week
    b. three days
    c. two days
    d. five days

6. What vitamin did Sam lack?
    a. vitamin D
    b. vitamin A
    c. vitamin C
    d. vitamin E

My Side of the Mountain Study/Quiz Questions Multiple Choice Format Page 14

7. Sam helps the deer in January by
    a. shelling acorns for them.
    b. cutting tender branches for them to eat.
    c. setting up a salt lick.
    d. making a shelter from the snow for them.

My Side of the Mountain Study/Quiz Questions Multiple Choice Format Page 15

Set #8 "The Spring in the Winter and the Beginning of My Story's End", "I Cooperate with the Ending", "The City Comes to Me"

1. It takes _____ cups of sap to make one cup of syrup.
    a. 40
    b. 10
    c. 32
    d. 23

2. Matt Spell is
    a. a reporter looking for the wild boy.
    b. a young man from town.
    c. a college professor on sabbatical.
    d. a songwriter from New York.

3. Sam refuses to make a deal with Matt Spell.
    a. true
    b. false

4. Sam is able to talk things out without anyone there to talk things over with because he
    a. holds forums among his friends and relatives in his head.
    b. remembers everything anyone ever told him.
    c. knows exactly what his friends would say if he asked them.
    d. uses his forest friends as an audience.

5. Aaron is
    a. a New York photographer.
    b. a reporter looking for the wild boy.
    c. a local boy looking for Daniel Boone.
    d. a New York songwriter.

6. Who else shows up to spend spring vacation with Sam?
    a. Bando
    b. Matt Speak
    c. his father
    d. Mr. Jacket

My Side of the Mountain Study/Quiz Questions Multiple Choice Format Page 16

7. Sam knows he is no longer a runaway because
    a. people are getting to know where he is located.
    b. he is getting company every day.
    c. Bando and Matt are making guest homes from other trees.
    d. his father knows where he is and comes to visit.

8. Who becomes a regular weekend guest?
    a. Daniel Boone
    b. Thoreau
    c. Bando
    d. Mr. Jacket (Tom Sidler)

9. Photographers shooting pictures of the wild boy show up intruding upon Sam's privacy.
    a. true
    b. false

10. The title of the last chapter "The City Comes to Me" means
    a. the photographers from the city are invading Sam's privacy.
    b. his family comes from the city to live in the woods with him.
    c. New York reporters are bringing in researchers from the city to examine Sam.
    d. New York nature lovers are flocking to the country to live like Sam.

ANSWER KEY - MULTIPLE CHOICE STUDY/QUIZ QUESTIONS
My Side of the Mountain

Set #1	Set #2	Set #3	Set #4
1. A	1. B	1. B	1. C
2. C	2. A	2. A	2. D
3. B	3. D	3. D	3. A
4. D	4. C	4. D	4. B
5. D	5. D	5. C	5. C
6. C	6. A	6. D	6. A
7. A	7. B	7. D	7. D
8. B	8. C	8. A	8. B
9. D	9. D	9. D	
10. D	10. A	10. A	
11. A	11. B		
12. D	12. B		
13. B			
14. A			

Set #5	Set #6	Set #7	Set #8
1. C	1. C	1. A	1. C
2. B	2. B	2. D	2. A
3. A	3. C	3. D	3. B
4. C	4. A	4. A	4. A
5. A	5. D	5. B	5. D
6. D	6. D	6. C	6. A
7. B	7. A	7. B	7. C
8. A	8. A		8. D
9. D	9. C		9. A
10. B	10. B		10. B

PREREADING VOCABULARY WORKSHEETS

VOCABULARY - *My Side of the Mountain*

SET # 1

Part I: Using Prior Knowledge and Contextual Clues

Below are the sentences in which the vocabulary words appear in the text. Read the sentence. Use any clues you can find in the sentence combined with your prior knowledge, and write what you think the underlined words mean on the lines provided.

1. Even the first night that I spent out in the woods, when I couldn't get the fire started, was not as frightening as the snowstorm that gathered behind the *gorge* and mushroomed up over my mountain.

2. Frightful seemed restless and pulled at her *tethers*.

3. Sometimes he would tell me about Great-grandfather Gribley, who owned land in the Catskill Mountains and *felled* the trees and built a home and plowed the land.

4. He had also given me a little purse to put it in, and some *tinder* to catch the sparks.

5. Ferns grew along its bank, and its rocks were *upholstered* with moss.

6. I chopped away until I found a cold white *grub*.

7. ,8. All the manuals I had read were very *emphatic* about where the fish lived, and so I had memorized this: "In streams fish usually *congregate* in pools and deep calm water."

9. I fell asleep in his rocking chair that was pulled up beside his big hot *glorious* wood stove in the kitchen.

10. I read somewhere that it has *combustible* oil in it that the Indians used to start fires.

Vocabulary - *My Side of the Mountain* SET #1 Continued

Part II: Determining the Meaning - Match the vocabulary words to their dictionary definitions.

___ 1. gorge   A. larva of insects
___ 2. tethers   B. wonderful
___ 3. felled   C. flammable
___ 4. tinder   D. padded
___ 5. upholstered   E. material used to catch a spark from a flint
___ 6. grub   F. gather
___ 7. emphatic   G. canyon
___ 8. congregate   H. definite
___ 9. glorious   I. chopped
___10. combustible   J. leashes

Vocabulary - *My Side of the Mountain* SET #2

Part I: Using Prior Knowledge and Contextual Clues

Below are the sentences in which the vocabulary words appear in the text. Read the sentence. Use any clues you can find in the sentence combined with your prior knowledge, and write what you think the underlined words mean on the lines provided.

1. "This must be the warbler *migration*," I said, and I laughed because there were so many birds.

___

2. One manual I had read said to watch what the birds and animals were eating in order to learn what is *edible* and nonedible in the forest.

___

3. I poked around the foundations, hoping to uncover some old iron *implements* that I could use.

___

4. Too many leaves had fallen and turned to *loam*.

___

5. Although Great-grandfather's farm was somewhat *remote*, still hikers and campers and hunters and fisherman were sure to wander across it.

___

6. Trying to get a place to rest it took time and got it more tired, and I really felt I was going in circles and wondered how *primitive* man ever had enough time and energy to stop hunting food and start thinking about fire and tools.

___

7. Two *sentinel* boulders, dripping wet, decorated with flowers, ferns, moss, weeds, everything that loved water-guarded a bathtub-sized spring.

___

8. That's how *citified* I was in those days.

___

Vocabulary - *My Side of the Mountain* SET #2 Continued

9. I was shaking from *exertion* and I was tired.

_____

10. I *wormed* forward, and wham!-something hit my shoulder.

_____

Part II: Determining the Meaning - Match the vocabulary words to their dictionary definitions.

   ___ 11. migration   A. loose soil
   ___ 12. edible   B. prehistoric
   ___ 13. implements   C. active effort
   ___ 14. loam   D. tools
   ___ 15. remote   E. acting as guards
   ___ 16. primitive   F. faraway
   ___ 17. sentinel   G. the act of leaving one region for another
   ___ 18. citified   H. able to be eaten as food
   ___ 19. exertion   I. having city habits
   ___ 20. wormed   J. crept

Vocabulary - *My Side of the Mountain* SET #3

Part I: Using Prior Knowledge and Contextual Clues

    Below are the sentences in which the vocabulary words appear in the text. Read the sentence. Use any clues you can find in the sentence combined with your prior knowledge, and write what you think the underlined words mean on the lines provided.

1. A *rumpus* arose in the darkness.

   _____

2. He stood his ground and *berated* me.

   _____

3. And so the Baron and I met for the first time, and it was the beginning of a *harassing* but wonderful friendship.

   _____

4. I poked a stick in the hole at the base of the rock trying to *provoke* him.

   _____

5. Someone was *poaching*, and he might be along is a minute to collect his prize.

   _____

6. She was *hypnotized*.

   _____

7. This much I knew: :in order to tan hide, it has to be *steeped* in tannic acid.

   _____

8. He was a *personable* little fellow.

   _____

Vocabulary - *My Side of the Mountain* SET #3 Continued

9. She was *preening* her now silver-gray, black and white feathers.

_____

10. It was *tedious* work, and in August when the acorns are ready, I found that they made better flour and were much easier to handle.

_____

Part II: Determining the Meaning - Match the vocabulary words to their dictionary definitions.

___ 21. rumpus   A. tiresome; boring
___ 22. berated   B. grooming
___ 23. harassing   C. pleasing; attractive
___ 24. provoke   D. soaked in liquid
___ 25. poaching   E. put in a sleeplike state
___ 26. hypnotized   F. illegal hunting
___ 27. steeped   G. stir in action
___ 28. personable   H. annoying; tormenting
___ 29. preening   I. scolded harshly
___ 30. tedious   J. uproar; loud noise

Vocabulary - *My Side of the Mountain* SET #4

Part I: Using Prior Knowledge and Contextual Clues

Below are the sentences in which the vocabulary words appear in the text. Read the sentence. Use any clues you can find in the sentence combined with your prior knowledge, and write what you think the underlined words mean on the lines provided.

1. It was cold water, I never stayed in long, but it woke me up and started me into the day with a *vengeance*.

_____

2. The Baron Weasel would pop up and glance *furtively* at us.

_____

3. I found some *sassafras* trees at the edge of the road one day, dug up a good supply of roots, peeled and dried them.

_____

4. The outlaw jumped back, then saw she was tied and said " And who is this *ferocious*-looking character?"

_____

5. I crawled into the store tree to get the smoked venison and some cattail *tubers*.

_____

6. "How would you know about a wood *pewee* in your business?" I grew bold enough to ask.

_____

7. "You are a murderer or a thief or a *racketeer*; and you are hiding out."

_____

Vocabulary - *My Side of the Mountain* SET #4 Continued

8. Bando got the fire hot by blowing on it with some homemade *bellows* that he fashioned from one of my skins that he tied together like a balloon.

_____

9. I sewed every free minute for four days, and when they were finished, I began a glove to protect my hand from Frightful's sharp *talons*.

_____

Part II: Determining the Meaning - Match the vocabulary words to their dictionary definitions.

___ 31. vengeance   A. tree with aromatic bark
___ 32. furtively   B. claws
___ 33. sassafras   C. a device for increasing the draft to a fire
___ 34. ferocious   D. fierce
___ 35. tubers   E. one engaged in illegal business
___ 36. pewee   F. secretly
___ 37. racketeer   G. small woodland bird
___ 38. bellows   H. underground stem which bears bud
___ 39. talons   I. revenge

Vocabulary - *My Side of the Mountain* SET #5

Part I: Using Prior Knowledge and Contextual Clues

Below are the sentences in which the vocabulary words appear in the text. Read the sentence. Use any clues you can find in the sentence combined with your prior knowledge, and write what you think the underlined words mean on the lines provided.

1. Sitting with her head under her wings, she was *toppling*.
___

2. The cold night air *revived* her.
___

3. I've got to *ventilate* this place.
___

4. The Baron chews with his back molars, and chews with a *ferocity* I have not seen in him before.
___

5. However, I did not *toy* with him.
___

6. I was *dismayed* to see what a mess my guests had made of my tree house.
___

7. They had found the *cache* of acorns and beechnuts and had tossed them all over my bed and floor.
___

8. ,9. It was a skunk! As I got used to the *indignity* and smell , I saw the raccoons *cavort* around my fireplace and dodge past me.
___

Vocabulary - *My Side of the Mountain* SET #5 Continued

Part II: Determining the Meaning - Match the vocabulary words to their dictionary definitions.

___ 40. toppling
___ 41. revived
___ 42. ventilate
___ 43. ferocity
___ 44. toy
___ 45. dismayed
___ 46. cache
___ 47. indignity
___ 48. cavort

A. brought back to a heathy state
B. frolic
C. safe hiding place
D. leaning over as if to fall
E. discouraged
F. play with; jest
G. fierceness
H. offensive to pride
I. allow fresh air to enter

Vocabulary - *My Side of the Mountain* SET #6

Part I: Using Prior Knowledge and Contextual Clues

Below are the sentences in which the vocabulary words appear in the text. Read the sentence. Use any clues you can find in the sentence combined with your prior knowledge, and write what you think the underlined words mean.

1. Her *plumage* had changed during the autumn, and she was breathtaking.

_____

2. I began to feel *conspicuous* and took the road to my mountain.

_____

3. Sometimes I would sit in my doorway, which became and entrance to behold- a *portico* of pure white snow, adorned with snowmen- and watch them with endless interest.

_____

4. "I see you have been busy. A blanket, new clothes, and an *ingenious* fireplace- with a real chimney-and say you have a silverware!"

_____

5. No *sensationalism* in this paper.

_____

6. "Then let us serenade the *conservationists* who have protected the American wilderness, so that a boy can still be alone in this world of millions of people."

_____

7. "I am pleased to meet the man who *sired* this boy."

_____

Vocabulary - *My Side of the Mountain* SET #6 Continued

8. Bando wanted to try some complicated jazz tunes, but the late hour, the small fire dancing and throwing heat, and the snow insulating us from the winds made us all so sleepy that we were not capable of more than a last slow *rendition* of taps before we put ourselves on and under skins and blew out the light.

_____

9. "What a *sanguine* smell. What a purposeful fire."

_____

10. He had some papers to grade, and he started off *reluctantly* one morning, looking very unhappy about the way of life he had chosen.

_____

Part II: Determining the Meaning - Match the vocabulary words to their dictionary definitions

___ 49. plumage   A. elaborate doorway
___ 50. conspicuous   B. noticeable
___ 51. portico   C. passionate
___ 52. ingenious   D. fathered
___ 53. sensationalism   E. feathers
___ 54. conservationists   F. clever; inventive
___ 55. sired   G. shocking material used to stimulate interest
___ 56. rendition   H. unwillingly
___ 57. sanguine   I. version
___ 58. reluctantly   J. those devoted to saving natural resources

Vocabulary - *My Side of the Mountain* SET #7

Part I: Using Prior Knowledge and Contextual Clues
Below are the sentences in which the vocabulary words appear in the text. Read the sentence. Use any clues you can find in the sentence combined with your prior knowledge, and write what you think the underlined words mean.

1. The wind howled, the snow *avalanched*, and the air creaked.
___

2. I considered him a pretty good *barometer*, and if he went to his tree early, I went to mine early too.
___

3. Caught in the act of *intruding*, he decided not to retreat, but came toward me a few steps.
___

4. He is *conserving* his energy, none of his flying around looking for food and wasting effort.
___

5. I made a fire, the tree warmed, and I puttered around with a *concoction* I called possum sop.
___

6. I overslept, I discovered, because I was in a block of ice, and none of the morning sounds of the forest *penetrated* my glass house to awaken me.
___

7. Now, I have seen ice storms, and I know they can be shiny and glassy and *treacherous*, but this was something else.
___

8. The rest were *resilient,* and unless a wind came up, I figured the damage was over.
___

Vocabulary - *My Side of the Mountain* SET #7 Continued

9. I *pondered* when I saw it, wondering if he had lacked a vitamin or two and had sought them in the bark.

_____

10. The deer could *forage* again.

_____

Part II: Determining the Meaning - Match the vocabulary words to their dictionary definitions.

___ 59. avalanched   A. entered
___ 60. barometer   B. extremely dangerous
___ 61. intruding   C. ability to recover rapidly
___ 62. conserving   D. gauge; standard
___ 63. concoction   E. search for food
___ 64. penetrated   F. thought over; mused
___ 65. treacherous   G. fell
___ 66. resilient   H. saving
___ 67. pondered   I. trespassing
___ 68. forage   J. mixture

Vocabulary - *My Side of the Mountain* SET #8

Part I: Using Prior Knowledge and Contextual Clues

Below are the sentences in which the vocabulary words appear in the text. Read the sentence. Use any clues you can find in the sentence combined with your prior knowledge, and write what you think the underlined words mean.

1. Then the activity gained *momentum*, and before I was aware of the change, there were the skunk cabbages poking their funny blooms above the snow in the marsh.
   _____

2. "I'm sort of an amateur *falconer*," I replied.
   _____

3. "And I think his shoes were just newspapers tied around his feet. That's good *insulation*, you know.
   _____

4. I sat down and listed some of the better wild plants and the more easily *obtainable* mammals and fish.
   _____

5. I was bigger and my hands were freer than his, so he *conceded* me the den.
   _____

6. I cooked supper, and then sat down by my little fire and called a *forum*.
   _____

7. Then Matt walked into the conversation and said that he wanted to spend his spring vacation with me, and that he promised no to do anything *untoward*.
   _____

8. That night I fell asleep with all these people discussing the *probability* of my being found and hauled back to the city.
   _____

Vocabulary - *My Side of the Mountain* SET #8 Continued

9. I was *self-sufficient.*

_____

10. Dad gave me a *resounding* slap and Mother hugged me until she cried.

_____

11. She got awfully mad at those newspaper stories *inferring* that she had not done her duty.

_____

Part II: Determining the Meaning - Match the vocabulary words to their dictionary definitions.

___ 69. momentum
___ 70. falconer
___ 71. insulation
___ 72. obtainable
___ 73. conceded
___ 74. forum
___ 75. untoward
___ 76. probability
___ 77. self-sufficient
___ 78. resounding
___ 79. inferring

A. gave in
B. able to secure
C. presuming; concluding
D. echoing
E. likelihood; chance
F. open discussion meeting
G. trainer of falcons
H. unfortunate
I. material used to retain heat
J. movement; speed
K. able to take care of self

ANSWER KEY - VOCABULARY
My Side of the Mountain

Set #1	Set #2	Set #3	Set #4
1. G	11. G	21. J	31. I
2. J	12. H	22. I	32. F
3. I	13. D	23. H	33. A
4. E	14. A	24. G	34. D
5. D	15. F	25. F	35. H
6. A	16. B	26. E	36. G
7. H	17. E	27. D	37. E
8. F	18. I	28. C	38. C
9. B	19. C	29. B	39. B
10. C	20. J	30. A	

Set #5	Set #6	Set #7	Set #8
40. D	49. E	59. G	69. J
41. A	50. B	60. D	70. G
42. I	51. A	61. I	71. I
43. G	52. F	62. H	72. B
44. F	53. G	63. J	73. A
45. E	54. J	64. A	74. F
46. C	55. D	65. B	75. H
47. H	56. I	66. C	76. E
48. B	57. C	67. F	77. K
	58. H	68. E	78. D
			79. C

DAILY LESSONS

LESSON ONE

Objectives
1. To give students background information for *My Side of the Mountain*
2. To give students the opportunity to fulfill their nonfiction reading assignment that goes along with this unit
3. To give students practice using library resources
4. To give students the opportunity to write to inform by developing and organizing facts to convey information.

Activity

Assign one of each of the following topics to a small group of your students or individually. Distribute Writing Assignment #1. Discuss the directions in detail. Take your students to the library so they may work on the assignment. Students should fill out a "Nonfiction Assignment Sheet" for at least one of the sources they used, and students need to submit these sheets with their compositions. Answer any questions they may have about filling out this form.

Topics:
1. Where are the Catskill Mountains located?
2. Research the specific bird life found in this locality.
3. Find out what animals would live in the Catskill Mountain area.
4. Identify the type of vegetation available in the Catskill Mountain area.
5. Discover the various land forms you may find in this type of geographical area.
6. Define the climate found in the Catskills.
7. State the distance between New York City and the Catskill Mountains.
8. What county in New York are the Catskills located?
9. Locate the nearest towns to the Catskills.
10. Discover the length and severity of the winters in this geographical area.
11. Determine what would be necessary for survival in this type of climate.
12. What well-known Washington Irving character is associated with these mountains?
13. What distances are Delhi and Poughkeepsie, New York from the Catskills?

WRITING ASSIGNMENT #1 - *My Side of the Mountain*

PROMPT

You are going to read an adventure of a young boy, Sam Gribley, who runs away to live in the wilderness. Before you read this fascinating tale of survival, it would help you to have some background information about the setting of this story.

You have been assigned a topic about which you must find information. You are to read as much as you can about that topic. During the next class session, you will be asked to share the information you discovered with the class. All class members will take notes on the various topics covered. Drawing from this information, you will relate what you have learned by writing a descriptive composition based on the Catskill Mountains' **plant life, wildlife, geography and climate**.

PREWRITING

You will go to the library. While you are there, use the library's resources to find information about your topic. Look for books, encyclopedias, articles in magazines- anything that will give you the information you require. Take a few notes as you read to help you remember the facts.

After you have listened to other class members share and you have gathered your information, make a little outline, putting your facts in order.

DRAFTING

You will need an introductory paragraph in which you introduce your topic.

In the body of your composition, put the "meat" of you research- the facts you found or heard- in paragraph form. Each paragraph should have a topic sentence (a sentence letting the reader know what the paragraph will be about) followed by an explanation, examples, or details. In this case, you need a separate paragraph for each of the subtopics mentioned above.

Write a concluding paragraph in which you summarize the information you found and conclude your report.

PROMPT

After you have finished a rough draft of your paper, revise it yourself until you are happy with your work. Then, ask a student who sits near you to tell you what he/she likes best about your work, and what things he/she thinks can be improved. Take another look at your composition keeping in mind your critic's suggestions, and make the revisions you feel are necessary.

PROOFREADING

Do a final proofreading of your paper double-checking your grammar, spelling, organization, and the clarity of your ideas.

NONFICTION ASSIGNMENT SHEET - *My Side of the Mountain*
(To be completed after reading the required nonfiction article)

Name _____ Date _____

Title of Nonfiction Read _____

Written By _____ Publication Date _____

I. Factual Summary: Write a short summary of the piece you read.

II. Vocabulary
   1. With which vocabulary words in the piece did you encounter some degree of difficulty?

   2. How did you resolve your lack of understanding with these words?

III. Interpretation: What was the main point the author wanted you to get from reading his work?

IV. Criticism
   1. With which points of the piece did you agree or find easy to accept? Why?

   2. With which points of the piece did you disagree or find difficult to believe? Why?

V. Personal Response: What do you think about this piece? OR How does this piece influence your ideas?

LESSON TWO

Objectives
1. To give students the opportunity to orally share their research on the Catskills
2. To provide students with note-taking skills
3. To check students' nonfiction reading assignments
4. To allow students class time to work on their first writing assignment of the unit under your supervision

Activity #1

(Prior to this lesson, post a large map of New York state on your bulletin board.) Ask students to get out their research findings from the previous lesson. One by one, allow each student to briefly share their findings. You may want to group together information on the various subtopics to help organization of students' note-taking. Remind students to take notes as the class shares their findings. An additional dimension to this lesson could be to have each student draw a simple graphic to represent their finding on the map. (i.e. mountains where they should located, tree figure for different trees, etc.) Collect their nonfiction summaries sometime during this class period.

Activity #2

Review Writing Assignment #1's directions in detail. Give students the remainder of this class period to work on this assignment. While students are working on this assignment, distribute/assign the books to students. Give them a due date, keeping in mind you will be passing out the graded copies during the upcoming writing conference to be held on Lesson 5 day.

LESSON THREE

Objectives
1. To introduce the *My Side of the Mountain* unit
2. To distribute books and other related materials
3. To do the prereading work for Set 1
4. To identify setting, point of view, and flashback
5. To model effective oral reading skills by reading aloud pages 3-9
6. To draw attention to the author's use of hand-drawn illustrations

Activity #1

Distribute the materials students will use in this unit. Explain in detail how students are to use these materials.

Study Guides Students should preview the study guide questions before each reading assignment to get a feeling for what events and ideas are important in that section. After reading the section, students will (as a class or individually) answer the questions to review the important events and ideas from that section of the book. Students should keep the study guides as study materials for the unit test.

Vocabulary Prior to reading a reading assignment, students will do vocabulary work related to the section of the book they are about to read. Following the completion of the reading of the book, there will be a vocabulary review of all the words used in the vocabulary assignments. Students should keep their vocabulary work as study materials for the unit test.

Reading Assignment Sheet You need to fill in the reading assignment sheet to let students know when their reading has to be completed. You can either write the assignment sheet on a side blackboard or bulletin board and leave it there for students to see each day, or you can "ditto" copies for each student to have. In either case, you should advise students to become very familiar with the reading assignments so they know what is expected of them.

Extra Activities Center The Unit Resource portion of this unit contains suggestions for a library of related books and articles in your classroom as well as crossword and word search puzzles. Make an extra activities center in your room where you will keep these materials for students to use. Bring the books and articles in from the library and keep several copies of the puzzles on hand. Explain to students that these materials are available for students to use when they finish reading assignments or other class work early.

Books Each school has its own rules and regulations regarding student use of school books. Advise students of the procedures that are normal for your school.

Activity #2

Have students examine the cover and look through the book. Have them turn to page 3. Read the first chapter, "I Hole Up in a Snowstorm" orally to them pointing out the use of first-person point of view, flashback, setting, and the author's personal hand-drawn illustrations.

Activity #3
Have students complete the prereading work for Set 1 of *My Side of the Mountain*. They should review the study questions and do the required vocabulary work. Assign the reading of the remainder of Set 1.

LESSON FOUR

Objectives
1. To review the main events and ideas from Set 1
2. To preview the study questions for Set 2
3. To familiarize students with the vocabulary in Set 2
4. To give students practice reading orally (Set 2)
5. To evaluate students' oral reading
6. To give students the opportunity to practice writing to express personal ideas

Activity #1
Discuss the answers to the study questions for Set 1 in detail. Write the answers on the board or overhead transparency so students can have the correct answers for study purposes. Note: It is a good practice in public speaking and leadership skills for individual students to take charge of leading the discussions of the study questions. Perhaps a different student could go to the front of the class and lead the discussion each day that the study questions are discussed during this unit. Of course, the teacher should guide the discussion when appropriate and be sure to fill in any gaps the students leave.

Activity #2
Give students about fifteen minutes to preview the study questions for Set 2 of *My Side of the Mountain* and to do the related vocabulary work.

Activity #3
Have students read Set 2 orally in class. You probably know the best way to get readers within your class; pick students at random, ask for volunteers, have students who have just read select another student, assign numbers to students and spin a spinner, or whatever works best for you. Complete the oral reading evaluation form that follows this lesson after listening to your students read. If students do not complete reading Set 2 in class, they should do so prior to the next class meeting

Activity #4
Distribute Writing Assignment #2 and discuss the directions in detail. Allow any remaining class time for students to begin the assignment. There will be time allotted in the next lesson for students to work on this assignment. Give them specifics of when final copies are due to you.

ORAL READING EVALUATION - *My Side of the Mountain*

Name _____ Class____ Date _____

SKILL	EXCELLENT	GOOD	AVERAGE	FAIR	POOR
Fluency	5	4	3	2	1
Clarity	5	4	3	2	1
Audibility	5	4	3	2	1
Pronunciation	5	4	3	2	1
_____	5	4	3	2	1
_____	5	4	3	2	1

Total _____   Grade _____

Comments:

WRITING ASSIGNMENT #2 - *My Side of the Mountain*

PROMPT

The novel, *My Side of the Mountain* is an example of a flashback. The first chapter starts out six months after Sam has left his New York apartment home while he is "holed up in a snowstorm.". In chapter two, Sam goes back to the beginning of his adventure and portrays his undertaking by leading up to the snowstorm where he started and then taking it even further through the next spring by the end of the book.

Your assignment is to create a narrative flashback of your own by starting with a recent event, and then through the use of a shift in time, return to an earlier event or scene about which you would like to write. This is to be a brief autobiographical narrative piece of writing.

PREWRITING

A good way to start is to think about your past. Perhaps look at photographs or talk to family or friends to help you think of an event you would like to write about. Jot down what that is on a piece of paper. Make notes about the details of your special scene or event: where, when, who, what, etc.

Now, stop and think of a logical place and time to begin your autobiographical flashback. It could be today, it could be a time or place that is somehow related to your special event that brings that event especially close to your thoughts. Jot down some notes about that time or place and your feelings and thoughts about it.

DRAFTING

You should begin your paper with an introductory paragraph giving your reader your current place and time, or the place or time you chose with which to begin your flashback . Use your notes about the details of your starting place to help you get started.

The body of your composition should contain the actual recounting of the event or scene from your past you have chosen to recreate. Take each subtopic that you jotted down and make each one into a topic sentence for a paragraph in the body of your composition. Fill in each paragraph by telling the details of the event you have selected to write about.

Write a final paragraph in which you wrap up your narrative by stating the significance of your choice.

PROOFREADING

When you finish the rough draft of your paper, ask a student who sits near you to read it. After reading your rough draft, he/she should tell you what he/she liked best about your work, which parts were difficult to understand, and ways in which your work could be improved. Reread your paper considering your critic's comments, and make the corrections you think are necessary.

Do a final proofreading of your paper double-checking your grammar, spelling, organization, and the clarity of your ideas.

LESSON FIVE

Objectives
1. To review the main ideas and events of Set 2
2. To give students time to work on Writing Assignment #2 in class
3. To evaluate students' writing
4. To have students revise their Writing Assignment 1 papers

Activity #1
Use the multiple choice format of the study guide questions for Set 2 as a quiz to check students' comprehension of these pages and to review the main ideas and events of Set 2. Exchange papers for grading. Discuss answers and make sure students take notes for studying purposes.

Activity #2
Review the directions for Writing Assignment #2 and have students work quietly at their desks independently while you meet each of them individually for a writing conference.

Activity #3
Call students to your desk (or some other private area) to discuss their papers from Writing Assignment #1. Use the following Writing Evaluation Form to help structure your conference. Give students a date when revisions are due.

WRITING EVALUATION FORM - *My Side of the Mountain*

Name _____ Date _____

Writing Assignment #____ for the *My Side of the Mountain* unit   Grade _____

Circle One For Each Item:

Description (paragraph 1)	excellent	good	fair	poor
Plans (body paragraphs)	excellent	workable	fair	not realistic
Conclusion	excellent	good	fair	poor
Grammar:	excellent	good	fair	poor (errors noted)
Spelling:	excellent	good	fair	poor (errors noted)
Punctuation:	excellent	good	fair	poor (errors noted)
Legibility:	excellent	good	fair	poor

Strengths:

Weaknesses:

Comments/Suggestions:

LESSON SIX

Objectives
1. To discuss the theme of survival and identify character traits necessary for survival
2. To examine Sam's problem-solving techniques
3. To do the prereading vocabulary work for Set 3
4. To preview the study questions for Set 3

Activity #1

In small groups have students brainstorm character traits Sam displays that allow him to survive as well as he does. After students have determined the necessary traits, place each of them in the center of a separate web on the chalkboard. List specific actions and behaviors of Sam that can be attributed to each trait on lines extending from each web. Allow full class participation and encourage note-taking. Have students discuss how they think they would have managed to survive in Sam's place. Have them determine what would have been their greatest obstacle; their greatest strength.

Activity #2

Returning to their small groups, challenge students to find **specific** examples of Sam's problem-solving. For example, Sam needed a home that could not be seen by hikers so he chose a tree in which he could remain anonymous or Sam was having difficulty hollowing out his new home so he recalled that Indians burnt out their canoes with fire, so he used the same technique. Record on copies of the following chart made by students on their notebook paper. Come back together as a class and have each group share

PROBLEM	SOLUTION
Sam needed a home that could not be seen.	He chose a huge hemlock tree trunk for his hidden home.

Activity #3

Have students spend any remaining time in pairs previewing the study guide questions and doing the prereading vocabulary work for Set 3. Assign reading of Set 3 by next class session.

LESSON SEVEN

Objectives
1. To review the main ideas and events of Set 3
2. To do the prereading vocabulary work for Set 4
3. To preview study guide questions for Set 4
4. To silently read Set 4

Activity #1
Hand out four little slips of paper or mini cards to each student that have the letters A,B,C, or D on them. A good idea is to use different color cards for each letter. Use the multiple choice study guide questions and answers on Set 3 for an oral review. Read the question (and/ or show it on the overhead). Then give students the four possible answers, labeling them A, B, C, or D (or show on overhead again). Students respond by holding up the card with what they think is the correct answer. This is one variety of Every Student Response. Remind students not to look at what others are holding up, but to simply display the card of their choice. This is a quick indicator of students' comprehension. You can make it somewhat different by requiring complete silence and having them read the questions silently from the overhead, or make it more mysterious (fun?) by blindfolding everyone and have them hold up a certain number of fingers per answer instead of using the cards.

Activity #2
Assign the prereading vocabulary pages, study guide questions and silent reading of Set 4. Students should work on this independently while you catch up with any student whose writing conference has not been held or that needs any special help.

LESSON EIGHT

Objectives
1. To review the main ideas and events from Set 4
2. To preview the study questions for Set 5
3. To do the prereading vocabulary work for Set 5

Activity #1
Discuss the answers to the Study Guide Questions for Set 4 like was done earlier in Lesson 4.

Activity #2
Have students spend approximately 10 minutes completing the prereading vocabulary work independently. Pass out plain paper for drawing, or use individual easels or slates. Have one of the partners sketch their impression of one of the vocabulary words within a limited amount of time. The other one is to guess which vocabulary word he/she is trying to picture. When the correct

word has been chosen, play turns to the other partner. Continue play until all vocabulary has been covered for Set 5. This is similar to the game Pictionary. It could also be done in small groups. If time allows review vocabulary from previous chapters.

Activity #3
Tell students to preview the study questions for Set 5 in remaining class time and read it before the next class session.

LESSON NINE

Objectives
1. To review the main ideas and events from Set 5
2. To preview the study questions for Set 6
3. To do the prereading vocabulary work for Set 6
4. To discuss the theme of companionship

Activity #1
Divide the class into two teams. Play a game like a spelling bee, but instead of spelling a word, students must answer one of the questions correctly. Using the study guide questions for Set 5 begin play. 1. Determine which team goes first. 2. Read one of the questions for one team member to answer. 3. If it was answered correctly, that team gets a point. 4. If it was not answered correctly, the other team gets a try at the same question. 5. Question goes back and forth until it is answered correctly. 6. Read another question, and repeat earlier play. 7. Continue until all questions for Set 5 have been answered correctly. 8. Reward winning team with some small prize or other incentive.

Activity #2
Individually, have students look over study guide questions for Set 6 and do prereading vocabulary work for Set 6. Assign reading of Set 6 to be done by next class session.

Activity #3
Show pictures of examples of activities someone is enjoying with a companion. Be sure to include a variety of activities with a variety of companions: pets, older people, peers, etc. Ask students what they think all the pictures have in common. Lead them to coming up with the word *companionship*. Allow students to define their concept of this word. Next, have them share examples of the types of companionship they seek and enjoy. Discuss Sam's need for this and how he coped with it. If time, have students sketch scenes from the book that depict Sam's various companions and their role in his survival.

LESSON TEN

Objectives
1. To review the main ideas and events from Set 6
2. To review vocabulary from earlier reading
3. To review the newspaper articles Bando brings Sam
4. To write original articles about the Wild Boy of the Catskills

Activity #1
Use the multiple choice format of the study guide questions for Set 6 as a quiz to check students' comprehension of these pages and to review the main ideas and events of Set 6. Exchange papers for grading. Discuss answers and make sure students take notes for studying purposes.

Activity #2
Have students review the prereading vocabulary work for earlier Sets. Use the matching section of the vocabulary pages as a springboard for a game similar to Concentration. Divide students into groups of four or five. Have students quickly copy the vocabulary words (divide the task into sections to expedite) and their clues on separate index cards. Turn them all over, after mixing them up. Have students in small groups take turns flipping over two of the cards. If they are a match, i.e. a vocabulary word matches with its meaning, they keep the pair and get another turn. Students may look at the vocabulary words in their sentences for contextual clues. Continue play until all cards are matched into sets. Play again, if time.

Activity #3
Reread together the New York newspaper articles Bando brings along with him at Christmastime on pages 120-123. Look at the headlines and how the articles are written. Look at some current newspapers and compare similar human interest articles. Allow students to work together with a partner of their choice to write an article about Sam, pretending they have had the opportunity of interviewing him for their article. If time allows, also have students make an illustration to accompany their article.

LESSON ELEVEN

Objectives
1. To introduce simile, personification, and metaphor as figures of speech
2. To distinguish between three different types of figurative language/ literary devices
3. To have students locate figurative language in the text
4. To create original figures of speech
5. To illustrate figurative language

Activity #1

Tell the class you are going to read a few sentences to them from their most recently read chapters in the book. Ask them to listen carefully and try to identify similarities between them or see if they can identify what they are examples of:

- Bando wanted to try some complicated jazz tunes, but the late hour, the small fire *dancing and throwing heat* made us too sleepy
- The forest would be *as quiet as the apartment house* on Third Avenue
- I kept cutting wood and piling it *like a nervous child biting his nails*
- and he vanished *like a magician's handkerchief*
- The light from my turtle *lamp casts leaping shadows*
- It is *as big as a pumpkin and as orange*
- The stars are *like electric light bulbs*

Most of these examples happen to be similes. Point out the use of *like* and *as* to create the comparisons. When ready, move on the Activity #2

Activity #2

Make three columns on the chalkboard labeling each one separately: simile, metaphor, and personification. Spend some time here instructing about the other two forms of figurative language. You could use specific examples from the following test, focusing on the ones from earlier chapters. Perhaps you could cite some examples from familiar songs. Ask why they think any author or lyricist would use them? Do they use them? Why? In what way does using them enhance speaking or writing or the understanding of each of these. As a whole group, have students give you examples they can think of and then have them locate a few in any part of the text they have read. Allow them to come to the board and write these under the correct heading. When you are satisfied with their ability to recognize them and differentiate between them, go to the next activity.

Activity #3

Divide the class into small groups of three or four. Have each group assign a recorder. Give them a couple of sheets of paper. Ask each group to locate as many of these figures of speech as they can from the text. They may be more successful in the portion they already have read, but it isn't necessary to limit them. Giving them a time constraint is an option. It could be a race, you are the judge. You may want to rule out using the ones that are posted on the board. It's up to you. There are an endless supply in every chapter. Wrap this activity up by having the group with the **most** read their list aloud. Decide as a whole group if indeed each one is correct. Have all groups check off the ones that are read that they also found. Allow every group to read any that have not yet been mentioned. You could give small treats for first, second, third place, etc.

Activity #4

Have students create one example of each type. They could be individual sentences or you could require them to write a short paragraph using all three. Base this on the ability level of your students and/or time. Create one together as a model. If time, have them illustrate it with original art work or magazine pictures. Save finished products for display. They could do this part as homework.

Activity #5

Assign the Set 7 prereading vocabulary work and study guide preview to be done prior to the next lesson.

NOTE: The following figurative language test is optional. You may want to use it right after instruction, later in this unit, or not at all. You may choose to use it only as a resource for this lesson. It contains examples from the entire book.

ANSWER KEY FIGURATIVE LANGUAGE TEST - *My Side of the Mountain*

I.
1. P
2. P
3. P
4. S
5. S
6. M
7. P
8. S
9. S
10. M
11. S
12. P

II. Answers will vary.

III. Creative response.

FIGURATIVE LANGUAGE TEST - *My Side of the Mountain*

Read the following examples of figurative language. Label each one separately with either an **S** for simile, **P** for personification, or an **M** for metaphor.

1. I think the storm is dying down because the tree is not crying so much. _____

2. When the wind really blows, the whole tree moans right down to the roots, which is where I am. ___

3. I was busy keeping the flames low so they would not leap up and burn the fish. _____

4. The water that day was as dark as the rocks. _____

5. They looked as wild as the winds that were bringing them. _____

6. That second night the fire was magic. _____

7. My big voice rolled through the woods. _____

8. They looked like pebbles beneath those trees. _____

9. I felt as cozy as a turtle in its shell. _____

10. The trees were giants- old, old giants. _____

11. She was as alert as a high tension wire. _____

12. I could see my heart lift my sweater. _____

II. List one example of your own for each type of figurative language. They can be original or from your favorite songs or poetry.

III. Illustrate your favorite example of figurative language from those listed.

LESSON TWELVE

Objectives
1. To review the main ideas and events in Set 7
2. To do the prereading vocabulary work for Set 8
3. To preview study questions for Set 8
4. To make predictions
5. To read Set 8 together aloud

Activity # 1
Select any one of the previous methods of reviewing the study guide questions for Set 7 used in earlier lessons or allow the students to devise a way to do it.

Activity # 2
In small groups have students do the prereading vocabulary and previewing of study guide questions. Have them make predictions as to the possible answers of the questions.

Activity # 3
Have students read Set 8 orally in class. You probably know the best way to get readers within your class; pick students at random, ask for volunteers, have students who have just read select another student, assign numbers to students and spin a spinner, or whatever works best for you. Complete the oral reading evaluation form that follows this lesson after listening to your students read. If students do not complete reading Set 8 in class, they should do so prior to the next class meeting

LESSON THIRTEEN

Objectives
1. To review the main ideas and events in Set 8
2. To discuss the theme of individuality

Activity # 1
Use the multiple choice format of the study guide questions for Set 8 as a quiz to check students' comprehension of these pages and to review the main ideas and events of Set 6. Exchange papers for grading. Discuss answers and make sure students take notes for studying purposes.

Activity # 2
Reread Bando's comments to Sam on page 168 about being different. Have students in small groups discuss what they think it means to be an individual. Do you have to be different to be an individual? Can an individual be part of a group? Is it a good thing to be different? or a not-so-good-thing? Are some people more individualistic than others? What makes them that way? After the small groups have finished their discussion have them present a skit that portrays their findings to the class. It doesn't have to be elaborate or fancy, just a simple portrayal of what they discovered about individualism.

LESSON FOURTEEN

Objectives
 To give students the opportunity to practice writing to persuade

Activity
 Distribute Writing Assignment #3 and discuss the directions in detail. Give students the remainder of the class time to work on this assignment.

LESSON FIFTEEN

Objectives
 1. To discuss the ideas and themes from *My Side of the Mountain* in greater detail
 2. To have students exercise their critical thinking skills
 3. To try to relate some of the ideas in *My Side of the Mountain* to the students' lives

Activity #1
 Choose the questions from the Extra Discussion Questions/Writing Assignments which seem most appropriate for your students. A class discussion of these questions is most effective if students have been given the opportunity to formulate answers to the questions prior to the discussion. To this end, you may either have all the students formulate answers to all the questions, divide your class into groups and assign one or more questions to each group, or you could assign one question to each student in your class. The option you choose will make a difference in the amount of class time needed for this activity.

Activity #2
 After students have had ample time to formulate answers to the questions, begin your class discussion of the questions and the ideas presented by the questions. Be sure students take notes during the discussion so they have information to study for the unit test.

LESSON SIXTEEN

Objective
 1. To complete discussions begun in Lesson 15
 2. To give students the opportunity to share their writing Assignments #2 or #3 with the class

Activity
 Since part of Lesson 15 was taken up with giving students time to formulate answers, you will probably need a substantial portion of this class period to complete your class discussions.

WRITING ASSIGNMENT #3 - *My Side of the Mountain*

PROMPT

Now that you have completed reading the novel you know that Sam's family comes to Bitter Mountain to live with him. His father claims that Sam's mother insists they build a house and Sam feels this will ruin everything. Sam has been living on his own in the wilderness for a year and can see no reason for that to change now.

In this writing assignment, pretend you are clever and ingenious Sam Gribley, survivor of the wilderness of the Catskill Mountains. Your objective is to convince your parents that you are fine and it is not necessary for them to move the whole family in from the city and build a house in your precious wilderness.

PREWRITING

To begin with, list any and all possible arguments you can think that you could use to support your stand. Decide which are your strongest justifiable arguments, and which are less substantial. Organize your points from weaker to strongest and jot down anything you can think of which will support or explain your arguments.

DRAFTING

Begin with an introductory paragraph in which you express your frustration and discontent with this new development and infringement upon your recent lifestyle. Follow that with one paragraph for each of the main points you have to support your argument to convince them to let you continue to live off the land on Bitter Mountain. Fill in each paragraph with reasons and feelings that support your main point. Then, write an ending paragraph that summarizes your frustration and need to be on your OWN as your final statement.

PROMPT

When you finish the rough draft of your paper, ask a student who sits near you to read it. After reading your rough draft, he\she should tell you what he\she liked best about your work, which parts were difficult to understand, and ways in which your work could be improved. Reread your paper considering your critic's comments, and make the corrections you think are necessary.

PROOFREADING

Do a final proofreading of your paper double-checking your grammar, spelling, organization, and the clarity of your ideas.

EXTRA DISCUSSION QUESTIONS/WRITING ASSIGNMENTS
My Side of the Mountain

Interpretive

1. From what point of view is the story told? How would it have changed the book if told from a different point of view?

2. Describe the setting. Was it an effective choice by the author?

3. Are any of the characters in *My Side of the Mountain* stereotypes? If so, explain the usefulness of employing stereotypes in the book. If they are not, explain how they merit individuality.

4. What are the main conflicts in the story, and how are they resolved?

5. What is foreshadowing? Give examples of foreshadowing used in *My Side of the Mountain*.

6. Give a complete character sketch of Sam Gribley.

7. Explain what flashback is. How was it used in this story?

8. Define the role of each of these characters: Bando, Tom Sidler, Sam's father, Frightful, and the Baron.

9. Find the climax in this novel. Summarize the events leading up to it, and the remaining events after it which lead to the resolution.

Critical

10. Explain the significance of the title "*My Side of the Mountain*".

11. Compare and contrast a young boy's life today with life in the 1950's.

12. Why did the majority of people aware of Sam's situation find it odd? Would people think it odd today? Why or why not?

13. Compare and contrast Sam and his father.

14. Why did Sam run away from home?

15. Describe Jean Craighead George's writing style. How does it and her illustrations influence your view of the story?

My Side of the Mountain Extra Discussion Questions page 2

16. Give a rationale for the author including " IN WHICH" prior to most chapter titles.

17. Trace the changes in Sam's behavior and attitudes as the year commenced.

18. What universal themes are present in *My Side of the Mountain*?

19. Is the story of *My Side of the Mountain* believable? Why or why not?

20. Why would Jean Craighead George choose to write a novel like this?

Critical/Personal Response

21. Why did Sam's mother disapprove of him living alone on the mountain? How did that differ from his father's reaction? Why? How would your parents feel if you did something similar? Explain.

22. Why does Bando call Sam, Thoreau? What is Bando saying to Sam about the struggle of being different on page 168?

23. Who is responsible for the end of Sam's isolated existence?

24. Which of Sam's acquaintances did you like the most? least? Give support for your answer.

25. How does Sam learn from his mistakes? Can you think of a time you were able to learn from a mistake? Explain.

26. Was Sam successful at his venture in the wilderness? Explain and support your answer. What kind of a wilderness dweller would you be?

27. In what way did Sam prejudge Bando? On what did he base his opinion? Have you ever made a judgment about someone that turned out to be incorrect like Sam did? Explain.

Personal Response

28. Suppose you had a friend who ran away from home and you had an idea where you could find him/her. Would you try to get him/her to come home? What would you do?

29. Sam held make-believe forums in his mind to work out his problems because he had no one to discuss them with. What would you have done?

30. What is the value of learning to live "off the land" ?

My Side of the Mountain Extra Discussion Questions page 3

31. Would you like to live in the wilderness like Sam? Explain why or why not.

32. Do you or someone you know have as many siblings as Sam did (8)? What is it like to live with a large family in a small living space?

33. Have you read any other novels by Jean Craighead George? Compare them to *My Side of the Mountain*. Will you read the sequel to this novel, *On the Far Side of the Mountain*? Why or why not?

Quotations
1. "That land is still in the family's name. Somewhere in the Catskills is an old beech with the name Gribley carved on it. It marks the northern boundary of Gribley's folly- the land is no place for a Gribley."

2. "Sam Gribley, if you are going to run off and live in the woods, you better learn how to make a fire. Come with me."

3. "That's just what I want. I am going to trap animals and eat nuts and bulbs and berries and make myself a house."

4. "Well, I declare. We have some very good books on plants and trees and animals, in case you get stuck."

5. "Now what are you doing up here all alone? A little fellow like you should not be all alone way up here on this haunted mountain."

6. "It's all right, they've gone. If you don't tell on me I won't tell on you."

7. "Am I dreaming? I go to sleep by a campfire that looked like it was built by a boy scout, and I awaken in the middle of the eighteenth century."

8. "Thoreau, my friend, I am just a college English professor lost in the Catskills"

9. "Hunters are excellent friends if used correctly. Don't let them see you; but follow them closely."

10. "Well, if it isn't Daniel Boone?"

My Side of the Mountain Extra Discussion Questions page 4

11. "You are from New York. I can tell the accent. Come on, now, tell me is this what the kids are wearing in New York now? Is this gang stuff?"

12. "I'm doing research. Who knows when we're all going to be blown to bits and need to know how to smoke venison."

13. "Sam, you need a haircut."

14. "I don't know whether to send you home to play with my kid brother or call the cops."

15. "It is winter. It is winter and I have forgotten to do a terribly important thing- stack up a big woodpile. Sometimes I wonder if I will ever make it to spring."

16. "I see you have been busy. A blanket, new clothes, and an ingenious fireplace-with a real chimney- and say, you have silverware."

17. "Just awful. Any normal red-blooded American boy wants to live in a tree house and trap his own food. They just don't do it, that's all."

18. "Let us serenade the ingenuity of the American newspaperman. Then let us serenade the conservationists who have protected the American wilderness, so that a boy can still be alone in this world of millions of people."

19. "I know you are there! I know you are there! Where are you?" I've been reading about you in the papers and I could no longer resist the temptation to visit you. I still can't believe you did it. I was sure you'd be back the next day."

20. "You're the wild boy, aren't you? I work after school on the Poughkeepsie *New Yorker*, a newspaper."

21. "She's marvelous. How she manages to feed and clothe those eight youngsters on what I bring her, I don't know; but she does it. She sends her love, and says that she hopes you are eating well-balanced meals."

22. "Wild boy! What a sanguine smell. What a purposeful fire. Breakfast in a tree. I toil from sunup to sundown, and never have I lived so well!"

23. "I'll save all the newspaper clippings for you, and if the reporters start getting too hot on your trail, I'll call the New York papers and give them a bum steer."

My Side of the Mountain Extra Discussion Questions page 5

24. "I'll make a deal with you. Let me spend my spring vacation with you and I won't print a word of it. I'll write only what you told me."

25. " You really want to be found, or you would not have told Matt all you did."

26. "I like that. Sing it again. Let me suggest a few changes. Mind if I use the hum hum hum dee dee part? What other songs are sung up here?"

27. "The main reason is that I don't like to be dependent, particularly on electricity, rails, steam, oil, coal, machines, and all those things that can go wrong."

28. "Let's face it, Thoreau; you can't live in America today and be quietly different. If you are going to be different, you are going to stand out, and people are going to hear about you, and, if they hear about you, they will remove you to the city or move the city to you and you won't be different anymore."

29. "When you are of age, you can go wherever you please. Until then, I still have to take care of you, according to all the law I can find."

30. "We are going to have a house. Your mother said she was going to give you a decent home, and in her way of looking at it, that means a roof and doors.

LESSON SEVENTEEN

Objectives
      To review all of the vocabulary work done in this unit

Activity
      Choose one (or more) of the vocabulary review activities listed below and spend your class period as directed on the activity. Some of the materials for these review activities are located in the Vocabulary Resource section of this unit.

VOCABULARY REVIEW ACTIVITIES

1. Divide your class into two teams and have an old-fashioned spelling or definition bee.
2. Give each of your students (or students in groups of two, three or four) a *My Side of the Mountain* Vocabulary Word Search Puzzle. The person (group) to find all of the vocabulary words in the puzzle first wins.
3. Give students a *My Side of the Mountain* Vocabulary Word Search Puzzle without the word list. The person or group to find the most vocabulary words in the puzzle wins.
4. Use a *My Side of the Mountain* Vocabulary Crossword Puzzle. Put the puzzle onto a transparency on the overhead projector (so everyone can see it), and do the puzzle together as a class.
5. Give students a *My Side of the Mountain* Vocabulary Matching Worksheet to do.
6. Divide your class into two teams. Use the *My Side of the Mountain* vocabulary words with their letters jumbled as a word list. Student 1 from Team A faces off against Student 1 from Team B. You write the first jumbled word on the board. The first student (1A or 1B) to unscramble the word wins the chance for his/her team to score points. If 1A wins the jumble, go to student 2A and give him/her a definition. He/she must give you the correct spelling of the vocabulary word which fits that definition. If he/she does, Team A scores a point, and you give student 3A a definition for which you expect a correctly spelled matching vocabulary word. Continue giving Team A definitions until some team member makes an incorrect response. An incorrect response sends the game back to the jumbled-word face off, this time with students 2A and 2B. Instead of repeating giving definitions to the first few students of each team, continue with the student after the one who gave the last incorrect response on the team. For example, if Team B wins the jumbled-word face-off, and student 5B gave the last incorrect answer for Team B, you would start this round of definition questions with student 6B, and so on. The team with the most points wins!
7. Have students write a story in which they correctly use as many vocabulary words as possible. Have students read their compositions orally. Post the most original compositions on your bulletin board.

LESSON EIGHTEEN

Objective
To review the main ideas presented in *My Side of the Mountain*

Activity #1
Choose one of the review games/activities included in the packet and spend your class period as outlined there. Some materials for these activities are located in the Unit Resource section of this unit.

Activity #2
Remind students that the Unit Test will be in the next class meeting. Stress the review of the Study Guides and their class notes as a last minute, brush-up review for homework.

REVIEW GAMES/ACTIVITIES - *My Side of the Mountain*

1. Ask the class to make up a unit test for *My Side of the Mountain*. The test should have 4 sections: matching, true/false, short answer, and essay. Students may use 1/2 period to make the test and then swap papers and use the other 1/2 class period to take a test a classmate has devised (open book). You may want to use the unit test included in this packet or take questions from the students' unit tests to formulate your own test.

2. Take 1/2 period for students to make up true and false questions (including the answers). Collect the papers and divide the class into two teams. Draw a big tic-tac-toe board on the chalk board. Make one team X and one team O. Ask questions to each side, giving each student one turn. If the question is answered correctly, that students' team's letter (X or O) is placed in the box. If the answer is incorrect, no mark is placed in the box. The object is to get three marks in a row like tic-tac-toe. You may want to keep track of the number of games won for each team.

3. Take 1/2 period for students to make up questions (true/false and short answer). Collect the questions. Divide the class into two teams. You'll alternate asking questions to individual members of teams A & B (like in a spelling bee). The question keeps going from A to B until it is correctly answered, then a new question is asked. A correct answer does not allow the team to get another question. Correct answers are +2 points; incorrect answers are -1 point.

4. Have students pair up and quiz each other from their study guides and class notes.

5. Give students a *My Side of the Mountain* crossword puzzle to complete.

6. Divide your class into two teams. Use the *My Side of the Mountain* crossword words with their letters jumbled as a word list. Student 1 from Team A faces off against Student 1 from Team B. You write the first jumbled word on the board. The first student (1A or 1B) to unscramble the word wins the chance for his/her team to score points. If 1A wins the jumble, go to student 2A and give him/her a clue. He/she must give you the correct word which matches that clue. If he/she does, Team A scores a point, and you give student 3A a clue for which you expect another correct response. Continue giving Team A clues until some team member makes an incorrect response. An incorrect response sends the game back to the jumbled-word face off, this time with students 2A and 2B. Instead of repeating giving clues to the first few students of each team, continue with the student after the one who gave the last incorrect response on the team. For example, if Team B wins the jumbled-word face-off, and student 5B gave the last incorrect answer for Team B, you would start this round of clue questions with student 6B, and so on.

UNIT TESTS

SHORT ANSWER UNIT TEST #1 - *My Side of the Mountain*

I. Matching/Identify

___ 1. Bando   A. Tom Sidler's nickname for Sam

___ 2. Daniel Boone   B. Source of lacking vitamin C

___ 3. Jesses   C. Carried Sam to Catskills

___ 4. Liver   D. Deerskin portal

___ 5. Thoreau   E. Sam's siblings' beds

___ 6. Sam Gribley   F. Author

___ 7. Craighead George   G. First man to help Sam

___ 8. Train   H. Tormenting weasel

___ 9. Woodstove   I. College English professor

___ 10. Moccasins   J. Bando's Christmas gift

___ 11. Hammocks   K. Tom Sidler

___ 12. Door   L. Mountain boy

___ 13. Bill   M. Frightful's leg straps

___ 14. Halloween Party   N. Sam fell asleep next to Bill's

___ 15. Delhi   O. Fire starter

___ 16. Frightful   P. Sam's falcon

___ 17. Baron   Q. Nearest town to Sam

___ 18. Matt Spell   R. Poughkeepsie reporter

___ 19. Mr. Jacket   S. Turned out differently than Sam planned

___ 20. Flint   T. Bando's nickname for Sam

My Side of the Mountain Short Answer Unit Test 1 Page 2

II. Short Answer

1. Why had the Gribley farm been abandoned?

2. How does Mrs. Turner help Sam?

3. What important information did Sam learn from a manual about the outdoors?

4. What puzzles Sam about animal trapping?

5. How does Sam train Frightful?

6. What was the primary problem Sam encountered while trying out his new clay furnace?

7. How does Sam save apples for the winter?

My Side of the Mountain Short Answer Unit Test 1 Page 3

8. Upon returning from town, what does Sam realize is the one thing he hasn't done to prepare for winter?

9. What news does Bando bring when he comes for his Christmas visit?

10. What is his father's reaction to his living situation?

11. What was the most disturbing part of the ice storm?

12. What vitamin did Sam lack and how did he get it?

13. How is Sam able to talk things out without anyone there talk to things over with?

14. How does Sam know he is no longer a runaway?

15. What does the title of the last chapter "The City Comes to Me" mean?

My Side of the Mountain Short Answer Unit Test 1 Page 4

III. Essay

    Trace the changes in Sam's behavior and attitudes as the year commenced. Use details from the story to support your answer.

My Side of the Mountain Short Answer Unit Test 1 Page 5

IV. Vocabulary

   Listen to the vocabulary words and spell them. After you have spelled all the words, go back and write down the definitions.

   1.

   2.

   3.

   4.

   5.

   6.

   7.

   8.

   9.

   10.

KEY: SHORT ANSWER UNIT TEST #1 - *My Side of the Mountain*

I. Matching/Identify

_I_	1. Bando	A.	Tom Sidler's nickname for Sam
_A_	2. Daniel Boone	B.	Source of lacking vitamin C
_M_	3. Jesses	C.	Carried Sam to Catskills
_B_	4. Liver	D.	Deerskin portal
_T_	5. Thoreau	E.	Sam's siblings' beds
_L_	6. Sam Gribley	F.	Author
_F_	7. Craighead George	G.	First man to help Sam
_C_	8. Train	H.	Tormenting weasel
_N_	9. Woodstove	I.	College English professor
_J_	10. Moccasins	J.	Bando's Christmas gift
_E_	11. Hammocks	K.	Tom Sidler
_D_	12. Door	L.	Mountain boy
_G_	13. Bill	M.	Frightful's leg straps
_S_	14. Halloween Party	N.	Sam fell asleep next to Bill's
_Q_	15. Delhi	O.	Fire starter
_P_	16. Frightful	P.	Sam's falcon
_H_	17. Baron	Q.	Nearest town to Sam
_R_	18. Matt Spell	R.	Pougkeepsie reporter
_K_	19. Mr. Jacket	S.	Turned out differently than Sam planned
_O_	20. Flint	T.	Bando's nickname for Sam

II. Short Answer

1. Why had the Gribley farm been abandoned?
    The farm had failed so his great-grandfather went to sea.
2. How does Mrs. Turner help Sam?
    She finds books and maps about Delaware County which include the Gribley farm.
3. What important information did Sam learn from a manual about the outdoors?
    Watch what the birds and animals are eating to learn what is edible and what is not.
4. What puzzles Sam about animal trapping?
    He can't believe animals don't question why delicious food is in such a ridiculous spot.
5. How does Sam train Frightful?
    She does not eat unless she first flies to Sam's wrist.
6. What was the primary problem Sam encountered while trying out his new clay furnace?
    It was ventilation. The fire took all the oxygen out of his tree home.
7. How does Sam save apples for the winter?
    He cuts them into slices and dries them on a boulder in the sun.
8. Upon returning from town, what does Sam realize is the one thing he hasn't done for winter?
    He hasn't stacked a big wood pile.

9. What news does Bando bring when he comes for his Christmas visit?
    There are newspaper clippings from New York newspapers.
10. What is his father's reaction to his living situation?
    He is thrilled, proud, and amazed with his son.
11. What was the most disturbing part of the ice storm?
    The sound of the exploding trees.
12. What vitamin did Sam lack and how did he get it?
    He was lacking vitamin C and got it by eating rabbit liver.
13. How is Sam able to talk things out without anyone there to talk things over with?
    He holds forums in his head with his dad and friends each giving him their advice.
14. How does Sam know he is no longer a runaway?
    Bando and Matt make a guest home from one of the other trees.
15. What does the title of the last chapter "The City Comes to Me" mean?
    His family comes from the city to live in the woods with him.

IV. Vocabulary
    Choose ten of the vocabulary words to read orally for the vocabulary section of this unit test.

SHORT ANSWER UNIT TEST 2 - *My Side of the Mountain*

I. Matching

___ 1. Catskills   A. Location of Gribley farm

___ 2. Eight   B. One of Sam's concoctions

___ 3. Delaware County   C. Sam's motto

___ 4. Might is Right   D. Sunlight benefit

___ 5. Mrs. Fields   E. 97- year-old strawberry picker

___ 6. Clay   F. Raccoon

___ 7. Barometer   G. Number of Sam's siblings

___ 8. Tannic Acid   H. Setting

___ 9. Possum sop   I. Helped Sam walk in winter

___ 10. Ice storm   J. Head chickadee

___ 11. Aaron   K. Address of New York apartment

___ 12. Mr. Bracket   L. Necessary in Sam's new clothing

___ 13. Fried chicken   M. Mother's specialty

___ 14. Mrs. Turner   N. Used library scissors to cut Sam's hair

___ 15. Jesse Coon James   O. Sam's fireplace material

___ 16. Snowshoes   P. Weather forecaster nuthatch

___ 17. Vitamin D   Q. New York songwriter

___ 18. Willow whistles   R. Starved the birds

___ 19. Pockets   S. Used to tan deerhide

___ 20. Third Avenue   T. Trombone-like instruments

My Side of the Mountain Short Answer Unit Test 2 Page 2

II. Short Answer

1. Relate Sam's first night in the woods.

2. Sam values which type of trees the most and how does he remember where they are located on the property?

3. Why does Sam choose a hemlock tree for his home?

4. Who surprises Sam as he is constructing his bed?

5. How does Sam learn to season his food?

6. How is Sam able to get a deer?

7. Why does Sam take away the first sparrow Frightful catches?

My Side of the Mountain Short Answer Unit Test 2 Page 3

8. Cite the change in Sam's feelings after his visitor leaves.

9. What was the primary problem Sam encountered while trying out his new clay furnace?

10. In what way did Sam's Halloween party backfire?

11. With whom in the forest does Sam compare his Third Avenue, New York neighbors?

12. Why does his father come back and leave by a different route?

13. Why does Sam say there is no such thing as a "still winter night"?

14. How does Sam help the deer in January?

15. Who becomes a regular weekend guest?

My Side of the Mountain Short Answer Unit Test 2 Page 4

III. Essay

Why does Bando call Sam, "Thoreau"?

What is Bando saying to Sam about the struggle of being different, an individual?

My Side of the Mountain Short Answer Unit Test 2 Page 5

IV. Vocabulary

　　Listen to the vocabulary words and spell them. After you have spelled all the words, go back and write down the definitions.

1.

2.

3.

4.

5.

6.

7.

8.

9.

10.

KEY: SHORT ANSWER UNIT TEST 2 - *My Side of the Mountain*

I. Matching

H	1. Catskills	A.	Location of Gribley farm
G	2. Eight	B.	One of Sam's concoctions
A	3. Delaware County	C.	Sam's motto
C	4. Might is Right	D.	Sunlight benefit
E	5. Mrs. Fields	E.	97-year-old strawberry picker
O	6. Clay	F.	Raccoon
P	7. Barometer	G.	Number of Sam's siblings
S	8. Tannic Acid	H.	Setting
B	9. Possum sop	I.	Helped Sam walk in winter
R	10. Ice storm	J.	Head chickadee
Q	11. Aaron	K.	Address of New York apartment
J	12. Mr. Bracket	L.	Necessary in Sam's new clothing
M	13. Fried chicken	M.	Mother's specialty
N	14. Mrs. Turner	N.	Used library scissors to cut Sam's hair
F	15. Jesse Coon James	O.	Sam's fireplace material
I	16. Snowshoes	P.	Weather forecaster nuthatch
D	17. Vitamin D	Q.	New York songwriter
T	18. Willow whistles	R.	Starved the birds
L	19. Pockets	S.	Used to tan deerhide
K	20. Third Avenue	T.	Trombone-like instruments

II. Short Answer

1. Relate Sam's first night in the woods.
    He was scared, tired, and very hungry. His fire failed and he chose the wrong place to bed.
2. Sam values which type of trees the most and how does he remember where they are located?
    He values the hickory, walnut and apple the most. He marks x's on his map he made of the property on his road map.
3. Why does Sam choose a hemlock tree for his home?
    He admires its size and location.
4. Who surprises Sam as he is constructing his bed?
    A little old lady looking for her annual strawberry patch.
5. How does Sam learn to season his food?
    He boils hickory sticks to get the salty residue for seasoning.
6. How is Sam able to get a deer?
    He dragged a dead deer shot by a hunter into the woods and covered it with hemlock boughs.
7. Why does Sam take away the first sparrow Frightful catches?
    If she gets in the habit of eating what she catches she'll go wild.

8. Cite the change in Sam's feelings after his visitor leaves.
    Sam is now lonesome for human contact.
9. What was the primary problem Sam encountered while trying out his new clay furnace?
    It was ventilation. The fire took all the oxygen out of his tree home.
10. In what way did Sam's Halloween party backfire?
    The animals took over.
11. With whom in the forest does Sam compare his Third Avenue, New York neighbors?
    He compares his former neighbors with the chickadees.
12. Why does his father come back and leave by a different route?
    He doesn't want anyone to track him and find Sam to spoil his lifestyle.
13. Why does Sam say there is no such thing as a "still winter night"?
    The trees cry out, winds scream, and animals scurry all through the night.
14. How does Sam help the deer in January?
    He climbed trees and cut down tender limbs for them to eat.
15. Who becomes a regular weekend guest?
    Mr. Jacket (Tom Sidler) comes up frequently to stay with Sam.

V. Vocabulary
    Choose ten of the vocabulary words to read orally for the vocabulary section of the test.

ADVANCED SHORT ANSWER UNIT TEST - *My Side of the Mountain*

I. Matching

___ 1. Catskills   A. Location of Gribley farm

___ 2. Eight   B. One of Sam's concoctions

___ 3. Delaware County   C. Sam's motto

___ 4. Might is Right   D. Sunlight benefit

___ 5. Mrs. Fields   E. 97- year-old strawberry picker

___ 6. Clay   F. Raccoon

___ 7. Barometer   G. Number of Sam's siblings

___ 8. Tannic Acid   H. Setting

___ 9. Possum sop   I. Helped Sam walk in winter

___ 10. Ice storm   J. Head chickadee

___ 11. Aaron   K. Address of New York apartment

___ 12. Mr. Bracket   L. Necessary in Sam's new clothing

___ 13. Fried chicken   M. Mother's specialty

___ 14. Mrs. Turner   N. Used library scissors to cut Sam's hair

___ 15. Jesse Coon James   O. Sam's fireplace material

___ 16. Snowshoes   P. Weather forecaster nuthatch

___ 17. Vitamin D   Q. New York songwriter

___ 18. Willow whistles   R. Starved the birds

___ 19. Pockets   S. Used to tan deerhide

___ 20. Third Avenue   T. Trombone-like instruments

My Side of the Mountain Advanced Short Answer Unit Test Page 2

II. Short Answer

1. Explain the significance of the title "*My Side of the Mountain*".

2. Compare and contrast Sam and his father.

3. What universal themes are present in *My Side of the Mountain*?

4. Is the story of *My Side of the Mountain* believable? Why or why not?

5. Who is responsible for the end of Sam's isolated existence?

My Side of the Mountain Advanced Short Answer Unit Test Page 3
III. Quotations: Explain the importance and meaning of the following quotations.

1. "Sam Gribley, if you are going to run off and live in the woods, you better learn how to make a fire. Come with me."

2. "Hunters are excellent friends if used correctly. Don't let them see you; but follow them closely."

3. "I don't know whether to send you home to play with my kid brother or call the cops."

4. "Let us serenade the ingenuity of the American newspaperman. Then let us serenade the conservationists who have protected the American wilderness, so that a boy can still be alone in this world of millions of people."

5. "Wild boy! What a sanguine smell. What a purposeful fire. Breakfast in a tree. I toil from sunup to sundown, and never have I lived so well!"

6. " You really want to be found, or you would not have told Matt all you did."

7. "Let's face it, Thoreau; you can't live in America today and be quietly different. If you are going to be different, you are going to stand out, and people are going to hear about you, and, if they hear about you, they will remove you to the city or move the city to you and you won't be different anymore."

My Side of the Mountain Advanced Short Answer Unit Test Page 4

IV. Vocabulary

    Listen to the vocabulary words and write them down. After you have written down all the words, write a paragraph in which you use all the words. The paragraph must in some way relate to *My Side of the Mountain*.

MULTIPLE CHOICE UNIT TEST 1 - *My Side of the Mountain*

I. Matching

___ 1. Might is Right   A. Sunlight benefit

___ 2. Mrs. Fields   B. 97- year-old strawberry picker

___ 3. Barometer   C. Head chickadee

___ 4. Tannic Acid   D. Sam's motto

___ 5. Possum sop   E. One of Sam's concoctions

___ 6. Aaron   F. Address of New York apartment

___ 7. Mr. Bracket   G. Used to tan deerhide

___ 8. Vitamin D   H. New York songwriter

___ 9. Willow whistles   I. Weather forecasting nuthatch

___ 10. Third Avenue   J. Trombone-like instruments

II. Multiple Choice

1. Sam is able to know the current date by
    a. using a sundial he found.
    b. looking at the pocket calendar he brought along.
    c. making notches in an aspen pole for each day since he left home.
    d. determining the position of the moon and stars.

2. Sam prepares for winter in the forest by
    a. learning how to make a fire.
    b. finding edible plants.
    c. trapping animals and catching fish.
    d. all of the above

3. The Gribley farm had been abandoned because
    a. it had failed and his great-grandfather went to sea.
    b. of the forest fire that destroyed the mountain.
    c. the Civil War had taken his great-grandfather away to war.
    d. none of the above

My Side of the Mountain Multiple Choice Unit Test 1 page 2

4. Which of the following items *didn't* Sam take with him on his journey?
    a. a penknife
    b. field guides
    c. a ball of cord
    d. money

5. Where does Sam write down the things he wants to remember?
    a. He writes on scraps of paper.
    b. He types it into his personal notepad.
    c. He jots it down on pieces of bark.
    d. Both A and C

6. Which set of adjectives best describe Sam's feeling about his first night in the forest?
    a. scared, tired, hungry
    b. excited, hungry, confident
    c. curious, tired, anxious
    d. nervous, exhausted, warm

7. What important information did Sam learn from a manual about the outdoors?
    a. How to determine the best place to make a bed.
    b. Watch what the birds and animals are eating to learn what is edible and what is not.
    c. The best way to make a fire in the forest.
    d. none of the above

8. Sam is able to cook the crow eggs he finds by
    a. putting them in the sun and baking them.
    b. sewing together a skunk cabbage leaf to form a cup and boiling the eggs in it.
    c. dropping them gently into the bubbling, hot spring water.
    d. scrambling them and frying them on a hot stone.

9. What puzzles Sam about animal trapping?
    a. He can't understand how to make the trap work properly.
    b. He can't believe the animals aren't suspicious about the delicious food found in silly places.
    c. He isn't sure where to place the traps.
    d. Both B and C

My Side of the Mountain Multiple Choice Unit Test 1 page 3

10. Sam is able to get a deer because
    a. the hunter lost the scent and went the wrong way.
    b. it fell into his trap right after it was shot by the hunter.
    c. the hunter shot two deer and forgot about the first one.
    d. he camouflages it with hickory boughs so the hunter can't find it.

11. How does Sam train Frightful?
    a. He throws food into the air for her to fetch.
    b. She must listen for his whistle before she lands.
    c. He counts to ten and then she must land on his shoulder.
    d. She does not eat unless she first flies to Sam's wrist.

12. Sam is relieved when his visitor leaves.
    a. true
    b. false

13. Sam gets clay for his fireplace home from the stream bank by
    a. loading up a wheelbarrow and wheeling it home.
    b. filling his pants and dragging them home.
    c. carrying handfuls back to a tree stump.
    d. cramming it in all his pockets and taking it along with him.

14. The moral of Sam's Halloween party was
    a. Don't feed wild animals.
    b. You never know what a weasel will do next.
    c. The full moon causes unearthly events.
    d. Skunks will appear when you least expect them.

15. Which of the following *doesn't* Sam do with his winter days and nights?
    a. ice fish
    b. hunt
    c. cook
    d. write music

16. Bando brings newspaper clippings of
    a. the wild boy living in the forest.
    b. the great New York City fire.
    c. the prediction of the upcoming blizzard.
    d. his academic award at the college.

My Side of the Mountain Multiple Choice Unit Test 1 page 4

17. Which set of adjectives best describe Sam's father's reaction to his son's adventure?
    a. worried, nervous, disappointed
    b. excited, thrilled, apprehensive
    c. proud, amazed, thrilled
    d. furious, agitated, worried

18. What vitamin did Sam lack?
    a. vitamin D
    b. vitamin A
    c. vitamin C

19. Sam is able to talk things out without anyone there to talk things over with because he
    a. holds forums among his friends and relatives in his head.
    b. remembers everything anyone ever told him.
    c. knows exactly what his friends would say if he asked them.
    d. uses his forest friends as an audience.

20. The title of the last chapter "The City Comes to Me" means
    a. the photographers from the city are invading Sam's privacy.
    b. his family comes from the city to live in the woods with him.
    c. New York reporters are bringing in researchers from the city to examine Sam.

My Side of the Mountain Multiple Choice Unit Test 1 page 5

III. Quotations: Identify the speaker:

A = Tom Sidler   B = Sam   C = Dad   D = Mom   E = Bando

F = Mrs. Turner   G = Frightful   H = Matt Spell

1. "Well, I declare. We have some very good books on plants and trees and animals, in case you get stuck."

2. "Am I dreaming? I go to sleep by a campfire that looked like it was built by a boy scout, and I awaken in the middle of the eighteenth century."

3. "Well, if it isn't Daniel Boone?"

4. "Let us serenade the ingenuity of the American newspaperman. Then let us serenade the conservationists who have protected the American wilderness, so that a boy can still be alone in this world of millions of people."

5. "I know you are there! I know you are there! Where are you?" I've been reading about you in the papers and I could no longer resist the temptation to visit you. I still can't believe you did it. I was sure you'd be back the next day."

6. "You're the wild boy, aren't you? I work after school on the Poughkeepsie *New Yorker*.

7. "Wild boy! What a sanguine smell. What a purposeful fire. Breakfast in a tree. I toil from sunup to sundown, and never have I lived so well!"

8. " You really want to be found, or you would not have told Matt all you did."

9. "The main reason is that I don't like to be dependent, particularly on electricity, rails, steam, oil, coal, machines, and all those things that can go wrong."

10. "When you are of age, you can go wherever you please. Until then, I still have to take care of you, according to all the law I can find."

My Side of the Mountain Multiple Choice Unit Test 1 page 6

IV. Vocabulary (Matching)

___ 1. Felled   A. Fierceness

___ 2. Ferocity   B. Stir to action

___ 3. Forage   C. Echoing

___ 4. Implements   D. Passionate

___ 5. Conspicuous   E. Chopped

___ 6. Obtainable   F. Search for food

___ 7. Combustible   G. Gather

___ 8. Edible   H. Tools

___ 9. Furtively   I. Scolded harshly

___ 10. Rumpus   J. Revenge

___ 11. Provoke   K. Noticeable

___ 12. Resounding   L. Able to be eaten as food

___ 13. Sanguine   M. Able to secure

___ 14. Congregate   N. Flammable

___ 15. Falconer   O. Discouraged

___ 16. Vengeance   P. Active effort

___ 17. Exertion   Q. Trainer of falcons

___ 18. Berated   R. Uproar; loud noise

___ 19. Dismayed   S. Unwillingly

___ 20. Reluctantly   T. Secretly

MULTIPLE CHOICE UNIT TEST 2 - *My Side of the Mountain*

I. Matching

___ 1. Daniel Boone   A. Source of lacking vitamin C

___ 2. Jesses   B. Tom Sidler's nickname for Sam

___ 3. Liver   C. Sam's siblings' beds

___ 4. Thoreau   D. Author

___ 5. Craighead George   E. First man to help Sam

___ 6. Moccasins   F. Bando's Christmas gift

___ 7. Hammocks   G. Tom Sidler

___ 8. Bill   H. Frightful's leg straps

___ 9. Halloween Party   I. Turned out differently than Sam planned

___ 10. Mr. Jacket   J. Bando's nickname for Sam

II. Multiple Choice

1. Sam decides to make his home out of
    a. the former foundation of his great-grandfathers farm house.
    b. an abandoned cave.
    c. a run down hunter's cabin.
    d. a huge hemlock tree trunk.

2. Sam prepares for winter in the forest by
    a. learning how to make a fire.
    b. finding edible plants.
    c. trapping animals and catching fish.
    d. all of the above

3. Sam traveled from New York City to the Catskill area by
    a. hitching rides on produce trucks.
    b. walking part of the way and running the rest of the way.
    c. riding on a Greyhound bus.
    d. taking a train.

My Side of the Mountain Multiple Choice Unit Test 2 page 2

4. How does Bill help Sam?
    a. He feeds Sam.
    b. He teaches Sam how to make a proper fire.
    c. He goes with Sam to be sure he can get along OK.
    d. Both A and B

5. Is Sam's second night in the forest *more* or *less* successful than his first night?
    a. more
    b. less

6. What important information did Sam learn from a manual about the outdoors?
    a. How to determine the best place to make a bed.
    b. Watch what the birds and animals are eating to learn what is edible and what is not.
    c. The best way to make a fire in the forest.

7. Why does Sam choose a hemlock tree for his home?
    a. He admires its size.
    b. He thinks no one would find him there.
    c. He is thrilled with its location.
    d. all of the above

8. Sam realized he can use fire like the Indians did to
    a. to send smoke signals in an emergency.
    b. to cook and smoke his animals and fish
    c. burn out the interior of his hemlock tree trunk home.
    d. all of the above

9. Sam takes away the first sparrow Frightful catches.
    a. true
    b. false

10. Bando uses the clay they find along the stream bank to
    a. make pottery in which to store their jam.
    b. make adobe bricks for a new home.
    c. form artistic sculptures of the animals in the forest.
    d. create a stove in which to bake acorn bread.

My Side of the Mountain Multiple Choice Unit Test 2 page 3

11. Select the one item not associated with Bando's wind whistles.
    a. They are trombone-like.
    b. They are made from willow reeds.
    c. They have a mouthpiece.
    d. They play sad songs best.

12. Sam's primary problem with his new clay furnace was
    a. getting the clay to stand up.
    b. keeping the ashes out of the way.
    c. ventilation.
    d. the size of the mouth.

13. Sam had a close call with the hunter because
    a. he was in the wrong place at the wrong time.
    b. Frightful drew the hunter's attention.
    c. he was confused and didn't know hunting season had started.
    d. his clothing resembled a deer.

14. Upon returning from town, Sam realizes he hasn't
    a. stacked a big wood pile.
    b. stored enough fruit.
    c. hidden his stash of food well enough.

15. Sam compares his Third Avenue, New York neighbors with whom in the forest?
    a. red-eyed vireos
    b. nuthatches
    c. squirrels
    d. chickadees

16. His father returns and then leaves by a different route because
    a. he forgot which way to go and needed Sam's help.
    b. he didn't want anyone following him.
    c. the storm caused the original route to be closed.

17. Name the animal that Sam called his barometer to the upcoming weather.
    a. red vireo
    b. chipmunk
    c. possum
    d. nuthatch

My Side of the Mountain Multiple Choice Unit Test 2 page 4

18. Sam says there is no such thing as a "still winter night" because
    a. the trees cry out
    b. the winds scream
    c. animals scurry
    d. all of the above

19. Sam helps the deer in January by
    a. shelling acorns for them.
    b. cutting tender branches for them to eat.
    c. setting up a salt lick.
    d. making a shelter from the snow for them.

20. Who becomes a regular weekend guest?
    a. Daniel Boone
    b. Thoreau
    c. Bando
    d. Mr. Jacket (Tom Sidler)

My Side of the Mountain Multiple Choice Unit Test 2 page 5

III. Quotations: Identify the speaker:

A = Dad   B = Mom   C = Matt Spell   D = Brando   E = Sam

F = Frightful   G = Tom Sidler   H = Mrs. Turner

1. "Well, I declare. We have some very good books on plants and trees and animals, in case you get stuck."

2. "Am I dreaming? I go to sleep by a campfire that looked like it was built by a boy scout, and I awaken in the middle of the eighteenth century."

3. "Well, if it isn't Daniel Boone?"

4. "Let us serenade the ingenuity of the American newspaperman. Then let us serenade the conservationists who have protected the American wilderness, so that a boy can still be alone in this world of millions of people."

5. "I know you are there! I know you are there! Where are you?" I've been reading about you in the papers and I could no longer resist the temptation to visit you. I still can't believe you did it. I was sure you'd be back the next day."

6. "You're the wild boy, aren't you? I work after school on the Poughkeepsie *New Yorker*, a newspaper."

7. "Wild boy! What a sanguine smell. What a purposeful fire. Breakfast in a tree. I toil from sunup to sundown, and never have I lived so well!"

8. " You really want to be found, or you would not have told Matt all you did."

9. "The main reason is that I don't like to be dependent, particularly on electricity, rails, steam, oil, coal, machines, and all those things that can go wrong."

10. "When you are of age, you can go wherever you please. Until then, I still have to take care of you, according to all the law I can find."

My Side of the Mountain Multiple Choice Unit Test 2 page 6

IV. Vocabulary (Matching)

___ 1. Bellows   A. Fierce

___ 2. Cavort   B. Fathered

___ 3. Ferocious   C. Gave in

___ 4. Forum   D. Likelihood; chance

___ 5. Ingenious   E. Device for increasing the draft to a fire

___ 6. Intruding   F. Faraway

___ 7. Personable   G. Version

___ 8. Sired   H. Tiresome; boring

___ 9. Revived   I. Frolic

___ 10. Talons   J. Pleasing; attractive

___ 11. Racketeer   K. Trespassing

___ 12. Tedious   L. Clever; inventive

___ 13. Rendition   M. Open discussion meeting

___ 14. Sentinel   N. Brought back to a healthy state

___ 15. Probability   O. Claws

___ 16. Remote   P. One engaged in illegal business

___ 17. Wormed   Q. Acting as guards

___ 18. Toy   R. Play with; jest

___ 19. Concoction   S. Mixture

___ 20. Conceded   T. Crept

ANSWER SHEET - *My Side of the Mountain*
Multiple Choice Unit Tests

I. Matching
1. ___
2. ___
3. ___
4. ___
5. ___
6. ___
7. ___
8. ___
9. ___
10. ___

II. Multiple Choice
1. (A) (B) (C) (D)
2. (A) (B) (C) (D)
3. (A) (B) (C) (D)
4. (A) (B) (C) (D)
5. (A) (B) (C) (D)
6. (A) (B) (C) (D)
7. (A) (B) (C) (D)
8. (A) (B) (C) (D)
9. (A) (B) (C) (D)
10. (A) (B) (C) (D)
11. (A) (B) (C) (D)
12. (A) (B) (C) (D)
13. (A) (B) (C) (D)
14. (A) (B) (C) (D)
15. (A) (B) (C) (D)
16. (A) (B) (C) (D)
17. (A) (B) (C) (D)
18. (A) (B) (C) (D)
19. (A) (B) (C) (D)
20. (A) (B) (C) (D)

III. Quotes
1. (A) (B) (C) (D) (E) (F) (G) (H)
2. (A) (B) (C) (D) (E) (F) (G) (H)
3. (A) (B) (C) (D) (E) (F) (G) (H)
4. (A) (B) (C) (D) (E) (F) (G) (H)
5. (A) (B) (C) (D) (E) (F) (G) (H)
6. (A) (B) (C) (D) (E) (F) (G) (H)
7. (A) (B) (C) (D) (E) (F) (G) (H)
8. (A) (B) (C) (D) (E) (F) (G) (H)
9. (A) (B) (C) (D) (E) (F) (G) (H)
10. (A) (B) (C) (D) (E) (F) (G) (H)

V. Vocabulary
1. ___
2. ___
3. ___
4. ___
5. ___
6. ___
7. ___
8. ___
9. ___
10. ___
11. ___
12. ___
13. ___
14. ___
15. ___
16. ___
17. ___
18. ___
19. ___
20. ___

ANSWER SHEET KEY - *My Side of the Mountain*
Multiple Choice Unit Test 1

I. Matching
1. D
2. B
3. I
4. G
5. E
6. H
7. C
8. A
9. J
10. F

II. Multiple Choice
1. (A) (B) ( ) (D)
2. (A) (B) (C) ( )
3. ( ) (B) (C) (D)
4. (A) ( ) (C) (D)
5. (A) (B) (C) ( )
6. ( ) (B) (C) (D)
7. (A) ( ) (C) (D)
8. (A) ( ) (C) (D)
9. (A) ( ) (C) (D)
10. (A) (B) (C) ( )
11. (A) (B) (C) ( )
12. (A) ( ) (C) (D)
13. (A) ( ) (C) (D)
14. ( ) (B) (C) (D)
15. (A) (B) (C) ( )
16. ( ) (B) (C) (D)
17. (A) (B) ( ) (D)
18. (A) (B) ( ) (D)
19. ( ) (B) (C) (D)
20. (A) ( ) (C) (D)

III. Quotes
1. ( ) ( ) (C) (D) (E) ( ) (G) (H)
2. (A) (B) (C) (D) ( ) (F) (G) (H)
3. ( ) (B) (C) (D) (E) (F) (G) (H)
4. (A) (B) (C) (D) ( ) (F) (G) (H)
5. (A) (B) ( ) (D) (E) (F) (G) (H)
6. (A) (B) (C) (D) (E) (F) (G) ( )
7. (A) (B) ( ) (D) (E) (F) (G) (H)
8. (A) (B) (C) (D) (E) (F) ( ) (H)
9. (A) ( ) (C) (D) (E) (F) (G) (H)
10. (A) (B) (C) ( ) (E) (F) (G) (H)

V. Vocabulary
1. E
2. A
3. F
4. H
5. K
6. M
7. N
8. L
9. T
10. R
11. B
12. C
13. D
14. G
15. Q
16. J
17. P
18. I
19. O
20. S

ANSWER SHEET KEY - *My Side of the Mountain*
Multiple Choice Unit Test 2

I. Matching
1. __B__
2. __H__
3. __A__
4. __J__
5. __D__
6. __F__
7. __C__
8. __E__
9. __I__
10. __J__

II. Multiple Choice
1. (A) (B) (C) ( )
2. (A) (B) (C) ( )
3. (A) (B) (C) ( )
4. (A) (B) (C) ( )
5. ( ) (B) (C) (D)
6. (A) ( ) (C) (D)
7. (A) (B) (C) ( )
8. (A) (B) ( ) (D)
9. ( ) (B) (C) (D)
10. ( ) (B) (C) (D)
11. (A) (B) (C) ( )
12. (A) (B) ( ) (D)
13. (A) (B) (C) ( )
14. ( ) (B) (C) (D)
15. (A) (B) (C) ( )
16. (A) ( ) (C) (D)
17. (A) (B) (C) ( )
18. (A) (B) (C) ( )
19. (A) ( ) (C) (D)
20. (A) (B) (C) ( )

III. Quotes
1. (A) (B) (C) (D) (E) (F) (G) ( )
2. (A) (B) (C) ( ) (E) (F) (G) (H)
3. (A) (B) (C) (D) (E) (F) ( ) (H)
4. (A) (B) (C) ( ) (E) (F) (G) (H)
5. ( ) (B) (C) (D) (E) (F) (G) (H)
6. (A) (B) ( ) (D) (E) (F) (G) (H)
7. ( ) (B) (C) (D) (E) (F) (G) (H)
8. (A) (B) (C) (D) (E) ( ) (G) (H)
9. ( ) (B) (C) (D) ( ) (F) (G) (H)
10. (A) ( ) (C) (D) (E) (F) (G) (H)

V. Vocabulary
1. __E__
2. __I__
3. __A__
4. __M__
5. __L__
6. __K__
7. __J__
8. __B__
9. __N__
10. __O__
11. __P__
12. __H__
13. __G__
14. __Q__
15. __D__
16. __F__
17. __T__
18. __R__
19. __S__
20. __C__

UNIT RESOURCE MATERIALS

BULLETIN BOARD IDEAS - *My Side of the Mountain*

1. Save a space for students' best writing. Make a nice border. Cut out letters KING OF THE MOUNTAIN or whatever title you want to show the meaning of the space. Staple up the best writing samples (or quizzes or whatever you have graded) on colorful paper.

2. Bring in (or have students bring in) pictures of outdoor life from magazines. Make a collage if you have enough different pictures (or post individual pictures on colorful paper if you only have a few pictures). This could also be a fun introductory activity if students participate. You could have the border and title done for the bulletinboard and invite students to staple up their own pictures wherever they want them. It will only take a few minutes of class time, but the students will enjoy it and you can get your bulletinboard done in a hurry.

3. Draw one of the word search puzzles onto the bulletinboard. (Be sure to enlarge it.) Write the key words to one side. Invite students to take their pens or markers and find the words before and/or after class (or perhaps this could be an activity for students who finish their work early).

4. Have artistic students create a mural depicting the various scenes from this novel or create a mural portraying just an overview of the wilderness area.

5. Students could write acrostic poetry using Sam's name or some other character's name as the basis. Display with illustrations of those characters.

6. Do a bulletinboard about companionship or individuality and use it as a springboard for further discussion.

7. Do a bulletinboard about careers available in agriculture or working with animals.

8. Portray and label the various wildlife and /or plantlife found on the mountain either through drawings or magazine pictures.

9. Create a large scale map and chart Sam's heroic journey from his Third Avenue, New York City apartment to the Catskills.

10. Post earlier written newspaper articles based on interviews with Sam.

11. Graphically have students compare their' daily lives with the daily life Sam lead in the wilderness.

EXTRA ACTIVITIES PACKET - *My Side of the Mountain*

One of the difficulties in teaching a novel is that all students don't read at the same speed. One student who likes to read may take the book home and finish it in a day or two. Sometimes a few students finish the in-class assignments early. The problem, then, is finding suitable extra activities for students.

One thing you can do is to keep a little library in the classroom. For this unit on *My Side of the Mountain*, you might check out from the school library other books by Craighead George. A biography of the author would be interesting for some students. You may include other related books and articles about survival in the wilderness, the Catskill mountain area, falcons, weasels, raccoons, plantlife, fishing, etc.

Other things you may keep on hand are puzzles. We have made some relating directly to *My Side of the Mountain* for you. Feel free to duplicate them for your students.

Some students may like to draw. You might devise a contest or allow some extra-credit grade for students who draw characters or scenes from *My Side of the Mountain*. Note, too, that if the students do not want to keep their drawings you may pick up some extra bulletin board materials this way.

The pages which follow contain games, puzzles and worksheets. The keys, when appropriate, immediately follow the puzzle or worksheet. There are two main groups of activities: one group for the unit; that is, generally relating to the *My Side of the Mountain* text, and another group of activities related strictly to the *My Side of the Mountain* vocabulary.

Directions for the games, puzzles and worksheets are self-explanatory. The object here is to provide you with extra materials you may use in any way you choose.

MORE ACTIVITIES - *MY SIDE OF THE MOUNTAIN*

1. Pick a chapter or scene with a great deal of dialogue and have the students act it out on a stage. (Perhaps you could assign various scenes to different groups of students so more than one scene could be acted and more students could participate.)

2. Have students design a book cover (front and back and inside flaps) for *My Side of the Mountain*.

3. Create a scrapbook like one Sam may have kept. Add real outdoor specimens if possible, labeled with short captions. Otherwise draw illustrations or cut out magazine pictures.

4. Have a guest speaker discuss the challenges of living off the land.

5. Use some of the related topics (noted earlier for an in-class library) as topics for research, reports or written papers, or as topics for guest speakers.

6. Research what careers are currently available for nature- lovers like Sam who do not want to be dependent on modern things.

7. If your school permits it, have a falconer come in with one or more falcons and give a demonstration.

8. Research the use of calendars. Keep a notched piece of aspen like Sam's during the course of reading this book. Make a notch for each day you are working on this unit.

9. Have students rewrite a section of the book as a play and act it out.

10. Try to make a willow whistle, as described on page 83.

11. Hold a discussion/workshop on the topic of "How to make and keep friends and still maintain your individuality."

12. Make blueberry jam like Sam and Bando did. Enjoy!

13. Try out some of Sam's recipes and report on which ones you like. Compare them to more traditional ones. How do they differ?

14. Work with clay to try to construct a fireplace like his.

15. Study about smoking meats and storing them for long periods of time. Report to the class.

16. Hold a Halloween party in honor of Sam's. Feed your wild animals!

PROJECT SURVIVAL - *My Side of the Mountain*

There are numerous true facts about nature and wilderness survival woven into Jean Craighead George's fictional adventure of Sam Gribley and his Catskill Mountain retreat. Students will create their own personal wilderness guide utilizing factual information from their novel.

Assignment 1   Divide the class into eight groups- one group for each section (set) of reading. Supply each group with chart paper. After rereading or skimming through their pages, each group's recorder should list the true facts related to survival they found in their pages on their chart paper.

Assignment 2   When all groups have finished, have a representative from each group share the information they were able to locate in their section of reading.

Assignment 3   Have each group decide which of the survival tips mentioned are the ones they find the most interesting. Vote within each group on which survival tips they will incorporate into their survival guide (if it is to be a group effort). (Guides can be a group effort, or an individual one)

Assignment 4 Using their chosen top seven to ten survival tips, students are to create a wilderness survival guide. They may use index paper, construction paper, or anything that is available to them. It should not only contain the facts, but illustrations, as well. When completed, display on a bulletin board or hang up around the room. These could all be a standard size, or you could allow the students creative license in determining the dimensions they would like them to be. They need to manageable in size to be useful. Encourage their use in the future by covering the outside pages with clear contact paper.

WORD SEARCH - *My Side of the Mountain*

All words in this list are associated with My Side of the Mountain. The words are placed backwards, forward, diagonally, up and down. The clues below the word search can help you find the words.

```
J Q K K X F B F G T V T N P C C A D B E R S G D
V G M T N E L R X N H T B R V D D A R J T S E S
W Z W O W N F P A G C G A T N S R A R I E L F Q
T Q R O Z V R I I C L C I N T O W T N O H S J Z
H A L L O W E E N S K C O M M A H F L I N T S S
B V N I L D C V T K A E A E L O M U I I E E V E
R D C N V I S H Y T P S T E R D F T M E L L C J
C E L H I E B T S K I E D E Z T V A X T L S O P
M L N L I C R K O S R B A H H R T Z S I I D R V
M O A R V C I P E V D U Z G Y I Q I R Y S U S L
N C C Y U L K O V P E O I F V L H P N P S T S T
C B J C L T H E J N D R O N S W A I T T E X K M
W P K S A S F H N N F N H R Q G A Q E K N J W R
B Y D K W S C R A I G H E A D R K K C A R O L S
B M T O Y S I B W B P W X X T T C A J E S S E S
W S N K J N X N Y L B L K S N O J N V Z P B S G
W S C F S J B H S V H H Y R P W H I T T L I N G
```

AARON	CRAIGHEAD	JACKET	SOP
APRIL	DANIEL	JESSE	SUIT
BANDO	DELAWARE	JESSES	TANNIC
BAROMETER	DELHI	KNIFE	THIRD
BARON	DOOR	LIVER	THOREAU
BILL	EIGHT	MATT	TRAIN
BITTER	FIELDS	MIGHT	TURNER
BRACKET	FLINT	MOCCASINS	VITAMIN
CAROLS	FRIGHTFUL	POCKETS	VOICE
CATSKILLS	HALLOWEEN	RACK	WHISTLES
CHICKEN	HAMMOCKS	SAM	WHITTLING
CLAY	ICE	SNOWSHOES	WOODSTOVE

KEY: WORD SEARCH - *My Side of the Mountain*

All the words in this list are associated with *My Side of the Mountain*. The words are placed backwards, forward, diagonally, up and down. The included words are listed below the word search.

```
                      B     T     T           A D B           D
                  N E   R     H     R       D A R J         E
              W O     F   A G   G A T       R A R I E L
          T     R O   V R I I   C I   T O W T N O H S
          H A L L O W E E N S K C O M M A H F L I N T S
          B   N I L D C   T K A E A E L O M U I I E E     E
          R   C N V I S       T   S T E R   F   M E L L
          C E   H I E B T S   I E D E   T   A   T L S O P
          M L N   I C R K O S R B A   H   T   S I I D
            O A R   C I   E V D U   G   I   I R       U S
              C Y U L K O     E O I   V   H P N   S T S
                C L T H E     D R O   W A I   T E
                  S A S     N N F     R     A   E K
                    W S C R A I G H E A D R     K C A R O L S
                      O   I B                 T   C A J E S S E S
                  N       N                   O J
              S                     S         P W H I T T L I N G
```

AARON	CRAIGHEAD	JACKET	SOP
APRIL	DANIEL	JESSE	SUIT
BANDO	DELAWARE	JESSES	TANNIC
BAROMETER	DELHI	KNIFE	THIRD
BARON	DOOR	LIVER	THOREAU
BILL	EIGHT	MATT	TRAIN
BITTER	FIELDS	MIGHT	TURNER
BRACKET	FLINT	MOCCASINS	VITAMIN
CAROLS	FRIGHTFUL	POCKETS	VOICE
CATSKILLS	HALLOWEEN	RACK	WHISTLES
CHICKEN	HAMMOCKS	SAM	WHITTLING
CLAY	ICE	SNOWSHOES	WOODSTOVE

CROSSWORD - *My Side of the Mountain*

CROSSWORD CLUES - *My Side of the Mountain*

ACROSS
1. Used to tan deerhide; ____ acid
5. Siblings' beds
8. First man to help Sam
9. Tormenting weasel
10. It; a particular one; point at ____
11. New York songwriter
12. Tom Sidler; Mr. ____
13. One of Sam's concoctions; possum ____
15. Item Sam took along with ice & $40
17. Thoughts
18. Remote Catskill retreat; ___ Mountain
21. Nearest New York town
24. Mountain boy; ___ Gribley
26. Sam's fireplace material
27. Automobile
28. Number of Sam's siblings
30. Sam's became rusty
31. Sound an owl makes
33. Rabbit fur-lined deerskin; winter ____
34. Carried Sam to Catskills
37. Sam fell asleep next to Bill's
39. Frightful's leg straps
40. Cowboy's compete & ride broncos in them

DOWN
1. Used library scissors to cut Sam's hair; Mrs. ____
2. Negative reply
3. Mother's specialty; fried ____
4. Fire starter
6. Poughkeepsie reporter; ___ Spell
7. Setting
8. Weather forecaster nuthatch
9. College English professor
11. Month to meet Matt Spell
12. Raccoon; ____ Coon James
14. Location of Gribley farm; ___ County
16. Starved birds; ___ storm
18. Head chickadee; Mr. ____
19. New York apartment; ___ Avenue
20. Built to smoke meat; smoking ____
22. Turned out differently than Sam planned; ____ party
23. Played on reed flutes; Christmas ____
25. Sam's code; ____ is right
29. Bando's nickname for Sam
32. Source of lacking vitamin C
33. Unhappy
35. Deerskin portal
36. Positive reply
38. Also

CROSSWORD ANSWER KEY - *My Side of the Mountain*

		T	A	N	N	I	C									F	
		U			O		H	A	M	M	O	C	K	S		B	I	L	L
B	A	R	O	N			I		A		A					A		I
A		N					C		T	H	A	T		A	A	R	O	N
N		E		J	A	C	K	E	T			S	O	P		O		T
D		R		E			E		D		K		R		M	
O				S		K	N	I	F	E		I		I	D	E	A	S
				S			C		L		L		L		T	
B	I	T	T	E	R		E		A		L		D	E	L	H	I
R		H		A		C			W		S	A	M		R		A
A		I		C	L	A	Y		A			I				L
C	A	R		K		R			R		E	I	G	H	T		L
K		D			V	O	I	C	E			H		H	O	O	T
E		L				L			S	U	I	T		O		W
T	R	A	I	N		S		D		A				R		E
		V		Y		W	O	O	D	S	T	O	V	E		E
	J	E	S	S	E	S		O			O		A		N
		R		S		R	O	D	E	O		U	

139

MATCHING QUIZ/WORKSHEET 1 - *My Side of the Mountain*

___ 1. Bando   A. Tom Sidler's nickname for Sam

___ 2. Daniel Boone   B. Source of lacking vitamin C

___ 3. Jesses   C. Carried Sam to Catskills

___ 4. Liver   D. Deerskin portal

___ 5. Thoreau   E. Sam's siblings' beds

___ 6. Sam Gribley   F. Author

___ 7. Craighead George   G. First man to help Sam

___ 8. Train   H. Tormenting weasel

___ 9. Woodstove   I. College English professor

___ 10. Moccasins   J. Bando's Christmas gift

___ 11. Hammocks   K. Tom Sidler

___ 12. Door   L. Mountain boy

___ 13. Bill   M. Frightful's leg straps

___ 14. Halloween Party   N. Sam fell asleep next to Bill's

___ 15. Delhi   O. Fire starter

___ 16. Frightful   P. Sam's falcon

___ 17. Baron   Q. Nearest town to Sam

___ 18. Matt Spell   R. Poughkeepsie reporter

___ 19. Mr. Jacket   S. Turned out differently than Sam planned

___ 20. Flint   T. Bando's nickname for Sam

KEY: MATCHING QUIZ/WORKSHEET 1 - *My Side of the Mountain*

_I_ 1. Bando   A. Tom Sidler's nickname for Sam

_A_ 2. Daniel Boone   B. Source of lacking vitamin C

_M_ 3. Jesses   C. Carried Sam to Catskills

_B_ 4. Liver   D. Deerskin portal

_T_ 5. Thoreau   E. Sam's siblings' beds

_L_ 6. Sam Gribley   F. Author

_F_ 7. Craighead George   G. First man to help Sam

_C_ 8. Train   H. Tormenting weasel

_N_ 9. Woodstove   I. College English professor

_J_ 10. Moccasins   J. Bando's Christmas gift

_E_ 11. Hammocks   K. Tom Sidler

_D_ 12. Door   L. Mountain boy

_G_ 13. Bill   M. Frightful's leg straps

_S_ 14. Halloween Party   N. Sam fell asleep next to Bill's

_Q_ 15. Delhi   O. Fire starter

_P_ 16. Frightful   P. Sam's falcon

_H_ 17. Baron   Q. Nearest town to Sam

_R_ 18. Matt Spell   R. Poughkeepsie reporter

_K_ 19. Mr. Jacket   S. Turned out differently than Sam planned

_O_ 20. Flint   T. Bando's nickname for Sam

MATCHING QUIZ/WORKSHEET 2 - *My Side of the Mountain*

___ 1. Catskills   A. Location of Gribley farm

___ 2. Eight   B. One of Sam's concoctions

___ 3. Delaware County   C. Sam's motto

___ 4. Might is Right   D. Sunlight benefit

___ 5. Mrs. Fields   E. 97- year-old strawberry picker

___ 6. Clay   F. Raccoon

___ 7. Barometer   G. Number of Sam's siblings

___ 8. Tannic Acid   H. Setting

___ 9. Possum sop   I. Helped Sam walk in winter

___ 10. Ice storm   J. Head chickadee

___ 11. Aaron   K. Address of New York apartment

___ 12. Mr. Bracket   L. Necessary in Sam's new clothing

___ 13. Fried chicken   M. Mother's specialty

___ 14. Mrs. Turner   N. Used library scissors to cut Sam's hair

___ 15. Jesse Coon James   O. Sam's fireplace material

___ 16. Snowshoes   P. Weather forecaster nuthatch

___ 17. Vitamin D   Q. New York songwriter

___ 18. Willow whistles   R. Starved the birds

___ 19. Pockets   S. Used to tan deerhide

___ 20. Third Avenue   T. Trombone-like instruments

KEY: MATCHING QUIZ/WORKSHEET 2 - *My Side of the Mountain*

H	1. Catskills	A. Location of Gribley farm
G	2. Eight	B. One of Sam's concoctions
A	3. Delaware County	C. Sam's motto
C	4. Might is Right	D. Sunlight benefit
E	5. Mrs. Fields	E. 97-year-old strawberry picker
O	6. Clay	F. Raccoon
P	7. Barometer	G. Number of Sam's siblings
S	8. Tannic Acid	H. Setting
B	9. Possum sop	I. Helped Sam walk in winter
R	10. Ice storm	J. Head chickadee
Q	11. Aaron	K. Address of New York apartment
J	12. Mr. Bracket	L. Necessary in Sam's new clothing
M	13. Fried chicken	M. Mother's specialty
N	14. Mrs. Turner	N. Used library scissors to cut Sam's hair
F	15. Jesse Coon James	O. Sam's fireplace material
I	16. Snowshoes	P. Weather forecaster nuthatch
D	17. Vitamin D	Q. New York songwriter
T	18. Willow whistles	R. Starved the birds
L	19. Pockets	S. Used to tan deerhide
K	20. Third Avenue	T. Trombone-like instruments

JUGGLE LETTER REVIEW GAME - *My Side of the Mountain*

SCRAMBLED	WORD	CLUE
ROANA	AARON	New York songwriter
ONDAB	BANDO	college English professor
EEAORRTBM	BAROMETER	weather forecaster nuthatch
ORNAB	BARON	tormenting weasel
LIBL	BILL	first man to help Sam
STKCSLLAI	CATSKILLS	setting
YALC	CLAY	Sam's fireplace material
EENNLDAIOBO	DANIEL BOONE	Tom Sidler's nickname for Sam
LEIHD	DELHI	nearest New York town
ODOR	DOOR	deerskin portal
THEIG	EIGHT	number of Sam's siblings
NIFTL	FLINT	fire starter
EEIICCFKRDHN	FRIED CHICKEN	Mother's specialty
HRUIGTFLF	FRIGHTFUL	Sam's trained falcon
CHOAMKSM	HAMMOCKS	siblings' beds
TRICESOM	ICE STORM	starved birds
SEESSJ	JESSES	Frightful's leg straps
VILRE	LIVER	source of lacking vitamin C
ALEMTPLST	MATT SPELL	Poughkeepsie reporter
HHGGIIITTSMR	MIGHT IS RIGHT	Sam's code
SSOACMCIN	MOCCASINS	Christmas gift for Bando
RRMTEABKC	MR. BRACKET	head chickadee
CRAKJETM	MR. JACKET	Tom Sidler
SSRMLIEDF	MRS. FIELDS	97 year old strawberry picker
RRRSTNEUM	MRS. TURNER	used library scissors to cut Sam's hair
STOEKCP	POCKETS	necessary in Sam's new clothing
OOSSSPMUP	POSSUM SOP	one of Sam's concoctions
MASYELBRIG	SAM GRIBLEY	mountain boy
KKMNOSGICRA	SMOKING RACK	built to smoke meat
SSSOOHNWE	SNOWSHOES	helped Sam walk in winter
AACCIIDNNT	TANNIC ACID	used to tan deerhide
EEUARHITDVN	THIRD AVENUE	New York apartment
REUOAHT	THOREAU	Bando's nickname for Sam
RANIT	TRAIN	carried Sam to Catskills
IIVMNATD	VITAMIN D	sunlight benefit
IIHWGTNTL	WHITTLING	hobby of Sam's
TTIIUSWNRE	WINTER SUIT	rabbit fur-lined deerskin
VOOOESDWT	WOODSTOVE	Sam fell asleep next to Bill's

VOCABULARY RESOURCE MATERIALS

VOCABULARY WORD SEARCH My Side of the Mountain

```
U B T I N D E R B F S P L O A M C
M P R A N R G L O R I O U S G B O
V Y H M L D F A L C O N E R R E N
F C M O V O I T R G R D X C U L C
T O P P L I N G O R G E D I B L E
R N R C L S P S N Y X R V T S O D
E S I A U T E F I P E H I T W E
A E N E M V M E R E T D H F V S D
C R G X T P O A R S L Y S I R E D
H V E E U R M R G E O L Y E G B D
E A N R B O E R T E D N E D N E L
R T I T E V N P E P R W A D D R P
O I O I R O T D O S R E Y B F A O
U O U O S K U M X R I E M B L T A
S N S N Z E M Z M C T L E O P E C
G I W W O R M E D F A I I. N T D H
G S A S S A F R A S C C C E I E I
K T C O N C O C T I O N H O N N G
T S F O R A G E S T E E P E D T G
```

BELLOWS	GLORIOUS	REMOTE
BERATED	GORGE	RESILIENT
CACHE	GRUB	REVIVED
CAVORT	INDIGNITY	SASSAFRAS
CITIFIED	INGENIOUS	SIRED
CONCEDED	LOAM	STEEPED
CONCOCTION	MOMENTUM	TALONS
CONSERVATIONISTS	PERSONABLE	TINDER
EDIBLE	PLUMAGE	TOPPLING
EXERTION	POACHING	TOY
FALCONER	PONDERED	TREACHEROUS
FELLED	PORTICO	TUBERS
FORAGE	PREENING	UPHOLSTERED
FORUM	PROVOKE	WORMED

VOCABULARY WORD SEARCH My Side of the Mountain

```
U     T  I  N  D  E  R           P     L  O  A  M  C
   P     A  N     G  L  O  R  I  O  U  S  G  B  O
      H     L  D  F  A  L  C  O  N  E  R  R  E  N
F  C     O     O  I  T           R  D     C  U  L  C
T  O  P  P  L  I  N  G  O  R  G  E  D  I  B  L  E
R  N  R  C  L  S  P  S  N  Y     R  V  T     O  D
E  S  I  U  A  U  T  E  F  I     E     I     W  E
A  E  N  E  M  V  M  E  R  T  D     F  V  S  D
C  R  G  X  T  P  O  A  R  S  L  Y  S  I  R  E  D
H  V  E  E  U  R  M  R  G  E  O  L     E     B  D
E  A  N  R  B  O  E  R  T  E  D  N  E  D     E
R  T  I  T  E  V  N  P  E  P  R     A  D     R  P
O  I  O  I  R  O  T     O  S  R  E     B     A  O
U  O  U  O  S  K  U        R  I  E  M     L  T  A
S  N  S  N     E  M        C  T  L  E  O     E  C
   I     W  O  R  M  E  D        A  I  I  N  T  D  H
   S  A  S  S  A  F  R  A  S        C  C  E  I  E  I
   T  C  O  N  C  O  C  T  I  O  N  H  O  N  N  N
   S  F  O  R  A  G  E  S  T  E  E  P  E  D  T  G
```

BELLOWS	GLORIOUS	REMOTE
BERATED	GORGE	RESILIENT
CACHE	GRUB	REVIVED
CAVORT	INDIGNITY	SASSAFRAS
CITIFIED	INGENIOUS	SIRED
CONCEDED	LOAM	STEEPED
CONCOCTION	MOMENTUM	TALONS
CONSERVATIONISTS	PERSONABLE	TINDER
EDIBLE	PLUMAGE	TOPPLING
EXERTION	POACHING	TOY
FALCONER	PONDERED	TREACHEROUS
FELLED	PORTICO	TUBERS
FORAGE	PREENING	UPHOLSTERED
FORUM	PROVOKE	WORMED

VOCABULARY CROSSWORD My Side of the Mountain

Across
1. prehistoric
5. movement; speed
6. underground stems which bear buds
8. clever; inventive
11. faraway
12. material used to catch a spark
13. play with; jest
14. larva of insects
16. safe hiding place
17. passionate
18. crawled
19. put into a sleeplike state

Down
1. entered in
2. trespassing
3. extremely dangerous
4. ability to recover rapidly
5. act of leaving one region for another
7. fathered
9. padded
10. revenge
14. canyon
15. loose soil
16. frolic

VOCABULARY WORD SEARCH KEY My Side of the Mountain

Across
1. prehistoric
5. movement; speed
6. underground stems which bear buds
8. clever; inventive
11. faraway
12. material used to catch a spark
13. play with; jest
14. larva of insects
16. safe hiding place
17. passionate
18. crawled
19. put into a sleeplike state

Down
1. entered in
2. trespassing
3. extremely dangerous
4. ability to recover rapidly
5. act of leaving one region for another
7. fathered
9. padded
10. revenge
14. canyon
15. loose soil
16. frolic

VOCABULARY WORKSHEET 1 - *My Side of the Mountain*

___ 1. Felled   A. Fierceness

___ 2. Ferocity   B. Stir to action

___ 3. Forage   C. Echoing

___ 4. Implements   D. Passionate

___ 5. Conspicuous   E. Chopped

___ 6. Obtainable   F. Search for food

___ 7. Combustible   G. Gather

___ 8. Edible   H. Tools

___ 9. Furtively   I. Scolded harshly

___ 10. Rumpus   J. Revenge

___ 11. Provoke   K. Noticeable

___ 12. Resounding   L. Able to be eaten as food

___ 13. Sanguine   M. Able to secure

___ 14. Congregate   N. Flammable

___ 15. Falconer   O. Discouraged

___ 16. Vengeance   P. Active effort

___ 17. Exertion   Q. Trainer of falcons

___ 18. Berated   R. Uproar; loud noise

___ 19. Dismayed   S. Unwillingly

___ 20. Reluctantly   T. Secretly

KEY: VOCABULARY WORKSHEET 1 - *My Side of the Mountain*

_E_	1. Felled	A. Fierceness
_A_	2. Ferocity	B. Stir to action
_F_	3. Forage	C. Echoing
_H_	4. Implements	D. Passionate
_K_	5. Conspicuous	E. Chopped
_M_	6. Obtainable	F. Search for food
_N_	7. Combustible	G. Gather
_L_	8. Edible	H. Tools
_T_	9. Furtively	I. Scolded harshly
_R_	10. Rumpus	J. Revenge
_B_	11. Provoke	K. Noticeable
_C_	12. Resounding	L. Able to be eaten as food
_D_	13. Sanguine	M. Able to secure
_G_	14. Congregate	N. Flammable
_Q_	15. Falconer	O. Discouraged
_J_	16. Vengeance	P. Active effort
_P_	17. Exertion	Q. Trainer of falcons
_I_	18. Berated	R. Uproar; loud noise
_O_	19. Dismayed	S. Unwillingly
_S_	20. Reluctantly	T. Secretly

VOCABULARY WORKSHEET 2 - *My Side of the Mountain*

___ 1. Bellows A. Fierce

___ 2. Cavort B. Fathered

___ 3. Ferocious C. Gave in

___ 4. Forum D. Likelihood; chance

___ 5. Ingenious E. Device for increasing the draft to a fire

___ 6. Intruding F. Faraway

___ 7. Personable G. Version

___ 8. Sired H. Tiresome; boring

___ 9. Revived I. Frolic

___ 10. Talons J. Pleasing; attractive

___ 11. Racketeer K. Trespassing

___ 12. Tedious L. Clever; inventive

___ 13. Rendition M. Open discussion meeting

___ 14. Sentinel N. Brought back to a healthy state

___ 15. Probability O. Claws

___ 16. Remote P. One engaged in illegal business

___ 17. Wormed Q. Acting as guards

___ 18. Toy R. Play with; jest

___ 19. Concoction S. Mixture

___ 20. Conceded T. Crept

KEY: VOCABULARY WORKSHEET 2 - *My Side of the Mountain*

E	1. Bellows	A. Fierce
I	2. Cavort	B. Fathered
A	3. Ferocious	C. Gave in
M	4. Forum	D. Likelihood; chance
L	5. Ingenious	E. Device for increasing the draft to a fire
K	6. Intruding	F. Faraway
J	7. Personable	G. Version
B	8. Sired	H. Tiresome; boring
N	9. Revived	I. Frolic
O	10. Talons	J. Pleasing; attractive
P	11. Racketeer	K. Trespassing
H	12. Tedious	L. Clever; inventive
G	13. Rendition	M. Open discussion meeting
Q	14. Sentinel	N. Brought back to a healthy state
D	15. Probability	O. Claws
F	16. Remote	P. One engaged in illegal business
T	17. Wormed	Q. Acting as guards
R	18. Toy	R. Play with; jest
S	19. Concoction	S. Mixture
C	20. Conceded	T. Crept

VOCABULARY JUGGLE LETTER REVIEW GAME CLUES - *My Side of the Mountain*

SCRAMBLED	WORD	CLUE
DEAAAHCLVN	AVALANCHED	fell
EERROMABT	BAROMETER	gauge; standard
EEDRBAT	BERATED	scolded harshly
ACCEH	CACHE	safe hiding place
TROVCA	CAVORT	frolic
IIFEDCTI	CITIFIED	having city habits
EEDDCCNO	CONCEDED	gave in
AEIYDDSM	DISMAYED	discouraged
LEEBID	EDIBLE	able to be eaten as food
CHATEMPI	EMPHATIC	definitely
NIOEEXRT	EXERTION	active effort
EEDLEFL	FELLED	chopped
EAROGF	FORAGE	search for food
UOMFR	FORUM	open discussion meeting
GRGOE	GORGE	canyon
BRUG	GRUB	larva of insects
SHSRAAGNI	HARASSING	annoying; tormenting
IIRRNNGEF	INFERRING	presuming; concluding
NNIIEGUSO	INGENIOUS	clever; inventive
ALOM	LOAM	loose soil
NMMMOEUT	MOMENTUM	movement; speed
BBOEAATINL	OBTAINABLE	able to secure
EEEATTNPRD	PENETRATED	entered in
GLEAMUP	PLUMAGE	feathers
PHIGNCOA	POACHING	illegal hunting
IIIEMTVPR	PRIMITIVE	prehistoric
OOKRPVE	PROVOKE	stir to action
EETMRO	REMOTE	faraway
UURMSP	RUMPUS	uproar; loud noise
SSSSAAARF	SASSAFRAS	tree with aromatic bark
DRISE	SIRED	fathered
OTY	TOY	play with; jest